Action Has No Season 2.0

How the Actionaire Develops
All Possibilities

Michael V Roberts, JD

authorHOUSE

AuthorHouse™
1663 Liberty Drive
Bloomington, IN 47403
www.authorhouse.com
Phone: 1 (800) 839-8640

© 2019 Michael V Roberts, JD. All rights reserved.
Front & Back Cover Design: Tanise A. Anderson
Edited by & Interior Graphics/Art Credit: Tamika A. Anderson, D.Sc.
Edited by: The Roberts Publishing Company
Edited by: Fallon G. Roberts, J.D. and Meaghan Johnson, J.D.

No part of this book may be reproduced, stored in a retrieval system, or transmitted by any means without the written permission of the author.

Published by AuthorHouse 10/04/2019

ISBN: 978-1-7283-2807-2 (sc)
ISBN: 978-1-7283-2805-8 (hc)
ISBN: 978-1-7283-2806-5 (e)

Library of Congress Control Number: 2019914502

Print information available on the last page.

Any people depicted in stock imagery provided by Getty Images are models, and such images are being used for illustrative purposes only.
Certain stock imagery © Getty Images.

This book is printed on acid-free paper.

Because of the dynamic nature of the Internet, any web addresses or links contained in this book may have changed since publication and may no longer be valid. The views expressed in this work are solely those of the author and do not necessarily reflect the views of the publisher, and the publisher hereby disclaims any responsibility for them.

TABLE OF CONTENTS

Foreword vii

Introduction xi

Chapter 1
    Predicament Solving 1
Chapter 2
    Time Management 12
Chapter 3
    Believe In Yourself 18
Chapter 4
    Inner City Innovation Centers 23
Chapter 5
    Inspiration To Act 28
Chapter 6
    An Achiever's Mindset 37
Chapter 7
    Attitude Control 44
Chapter 8
    Life's Transformations 51
Chapter 9
    Repositioning Yourself 57
Chapter 10
    Live With Expectancy 62
Chapter 11
    Get On The Right Track 66

Chapter 12
> Build Your Own Fence 72

Chapter 13
> Human Technology..83

Chapter 14
> Bartering To Cryptocurrency 95

Final Thoughts 103

About The Author 109

Prosperity & Abundance.. 117

FOREWORD

I am excited to write this foreword, not only because Michael V. Roberts Sr. is my father, but he is also my friend and my mentor and I deeply believe in the educative value of developing as an Actionaire for all leaders, entrepreneurs, and progressive thinkers, especially in a technology driven society. I also believe that Actionaires at every level and stage can enrich and strengthen their business and personal life by learning and understanding the principles and practices presented in this book. Taking Action can help Actionaires and leaders alike, learn to use their minds with power and skill.

My father introduced me to the concept of what it means to be an Actionaire during my years at Morehouse College. In the summers, I always worked at one of the family companies. The one summer I pledged and was inducted into the Kappa Alpha Psi Fraternity, being an Actionaire crystallized in my thoughts and I totally embraced my dad's philosophy. Consider *why* Actionaires succeed: they have a great vision, big dreams, high aspirations, lofty goals and they MUST take Action. Such ideas demand insight and strategy—and these are not simple things to learn & execute on your own.

That's precisely where this book comes in. It's a collection of strategies, yes – but strategies designed to create an understanding. Anyone can put together a random collection of stories. But my father's experiences and the lessons he shares in this book, take you deep inside of the business life of a successful Actionaire and will help you understand how to develop infinite possibilities for your personal life and business. That's what makes this carefully written book so special; it pays homage to the true nature of what it means to live fearlessly by giving Actionaires the guidance they need to see their vision and business through fresh eyes.

You can safely venture to say that any genuinely thoughtful book on Entrepreneurship and Leadership captures my attention. After all, I grew up in a home where I witnessed and experienced firsthand the implementation of these principles and practices from my father. It became apparent in my teenage years that the real destiny of an Actionaire was to influence others and achieve results through Action. The Actionaire lays the foundation of their future vision by setting goals, having the courage to take risks, and by showing others through their Actions that nothing and no one can stand in their way of accomplishing their mission. In this book, *Action Has No Season 2.0: How the Actionaire Develops All Possibilities*, you will gain a fresh new perspective on how to reposition yourself, how to live with expectancy, what it means to build your own fence, and how you can develop all possibilities as a successful Actionaire.

The real life experiences that my father shares in this book will connect to so many underlying situations in your personal life and business making each lesson you encounter a more enlightened experience. These stories help the Actionaire face real-life situations with clarity, resilience, courage, fearlessness, tenacity, strategic thinking, and much more.

As you page through this book, here are just a few of the things you will notice and love. First, these stories, are real-life experiences and some faced with challenges. They are no small achievements, because anyone who has ever worked in commercial real estate will tell you, the red tape is no fun and being a visionary who is a progressive thinker often faces difficulties trying to get others to see the vision you are sharing. Sometimes being an Entrepreneur and Leader can feel heavy, lonely, and even feel like you're drowning at times. You might feel like you are drowning. But as my father reminds us, the "Actionaire is never afraid of drowning. An Actionaire knows how to walk on water". We need to remind ourselves that being an Actionaire begins with taking Action and in taking Action we conquer two things at once. One, we conquer any doubts that may have tried to sabotage our plans and two, we conquer our goals. As a result, the Actionaire feels a kind of power where fear, doubts, and self-sabotage is no longer a barrier.

You'll also notice a strong emphasis on technology and the importance of the Actionaire being non-resistant to change. I applaud this with my whole being. Many years ago, I recall my father speaking about how the way we use currency would change, it would look different from the normal dollar exchange that we're used to using to pay for our goods and services. As we can see today, cryptocurrency has made an impact on the global market for how we exchange currency to purchase goods and services.

As Actionaires, we don't want to be left behind. We want to stay abreast on the new technology that's introduced to the market. We want to be ready to change with the trends and have fresh and innovative ideas to build upon. This book shows us how to do this.

It is filled with examples of powerful stories that demonstrate how to confidently embrace change and challenges.

Throughout this book, my father shares his wisdom about how he became an Actionaire and how you too can develop the skills and tenacity to achieve all of the possibilities of an Actionaire. Though every experience is different, you'll find the fabric of taking Action woven all through this text. It is the key to getting sustainable results. Consistency and Action are key components for the Actionaire. Leaf through the book to rediscover the impact of your mission, your message, and your movement. Share your vision with the people you trust. Work with a group of peers who share your vision and interact with those with whom you can help each other reach individual and collective goals. This is particularly important because it can help you gain clarity around your purpose.

Being an Actionaire is rewarding, freeing, and highly important. A book like this matters because it teaches us, how to do something that is both challenging and constructive. It teaches us to build a level of confidence that with time becomes unshakable. Thank you Dad for sharing so many lessons that drive us all to take Action that makes us look and feel more courageous each day! Because of you, we are proud to be Actionaires!

Michael V. Roberts, Jr.

INTRODUCTION

The Actionaire enjoys nothing more than to see people succeed with their business and personal endeavors. They understand the principle that a great leader does not merely create followers, rather they create more great leaders.

We hold dear to our hearts our dreams, goals, plans, passions, and wishes. Succeeding occurs only when we take Action and like an artist placing images on canvases, so does an Actionaire moving on their dreams, ideas, and aspirations. The Actionaire takes them on with courage, confidence, and bravado. This is the secret to happiness. Exploring Action develops the possibilities within your lifetime.

As a part of your efforts to reach your possibilities, the manifestation of certain principles is required. These principles will assist you in the development of a quality lifestyle. Winning requires a variety of skills and principles. Winners are those who have tried and lost but did not quit or give in to the temptation of being perceived as a failure.

The day you realize that there is no such thing as failure, is the day you become a true champion. Why do I say that? I say to you there is no such thing as failure, only experiences where the outcome wasn't as you would have liked. Rather, it is a gainful exercise that will only strengthen you in the future.

Becoming a champion doesn't begin around you; it starts inside of you. In your mind, is where you will begin to experience the happiness of a winner! In your mind, you will frame your future.

I wrote this book to be the second phase of my first book *Action Has No Season: Strategies and Secrets to Gaining Wealth and Authority*. It is to help the Actionaire grow into a fearless Capitalist. Capitalism leads to sustainable wealth and happiness.

The competitive prices and the distribution of goods and services are mainly determined by competing with those goods and services in that market. However, I believe the modern day capitalists must have a social agenda. I call that social capitalism. By that, I feel the capitalist must find ways to give back to the community it serves during its endeavors. Help the society through improving neighborhoods, schools, and health care.

The Actionaire's secrets to happiness are to embrace the wisdom and art of capitalism contained in this book. Capitalism is an economic system based on the private ownership of the means of production and distribution for profit. In a capitalist market economy, decision-making and investments are determined by every owner of wealth, property, or production ability in financial and capital markets. Prices and the distribution of goods and services are mainly determined by competition in these respective goods and services markets.

You must declare that the happiest and most productive days of your life are starting now! With 86,400 seconds in your day you must never, take your mind off of your mission. Why? Because some of your possibilities may be achievable within the next second on your existence.

I wrote this book for you. I believe that each page will give you the momentum and perspective you need to help you achieve your possibilities.

Chapter 1

PREDICAMENT SOLVING

In order to truly succeed and find happiness in life you must be willing to help yourself overcome tribulations. Actionaires are basically predicament solvers. A plumber solves problems, elected officials solve problems, a doctor, lawyer, and counselors solve problems. An Actionaire is an innovator, operating beyond a mere problem solver; more in line with a creator of new and expanding thought.

They select to live by choice and not by chance. They make changes, not excuses. They are motivated and not manipulated. The Actionaire is useful, but not used. They choose self-esteem over self-pity and never accept the opinions of random voices over their inner voice. If within your gut instincts or inner voice, you feel something is wrong, it probably is.

If you are to be an innovator, you must take inventory of yourself. What can you do that will be helpful to a customer or potential client? What do you enjoy doing? How innovative would you be if you could eliminate the fear of failure?

The fear of failure has no place in business. Believing in your instinct does have a place. If you have ever entered a room and felt rage in the air or walked into a place and felt positive energy and exhilaration that is instinct. An Actionaire feels an impulse or desire to get busy and makes time to pursue their dreams.

You will never be a capitalist or innovator unless you believe in the business or ideas you are promoting. Your attitude must always be in sync with your instinct. Doubting is a recipe for killing the possibility. If you have doubts, they will ultimately surface and may overtake your ideas. This will place you in a state of decline, ultimately causing the loss of your dream.

To succeed with your business, you must know your products and/or services. It will take time to perfect this knowledge. It might seem boring at times. You might think it is unnecessary. You might be anxious to sell your items, pocket the profit, and get on with your life. Sorry, true sustainable success does not happen without a serious "long term" commitment to excellence and accountability. You only have a chance of succeeding if you and your ideas have been vetted and thoroughly evaluated.

Are you spending the necessary time to expand your thoughts? How innovative are you? How much time do you spend cultivating an awareness of your possibilities? How many hours in the day do you invest in becoming informed of the possibilities? Are you too busy trying to make a fast dollar that you really have not developed a commanding perceptive and assurance in what you are attempting to accomplish? What is innovation?

Innovation is a new idea, creative thoughts, new imaginations in form of device of method. However, innovation is often also viewed as the application of better solutions that meet new requirements, unarticulated needs, or existing market needs. Innovation is related to, but not the same as invention. An innovation is more apt to provide a more creative application to an invention.

Always take time to focus internally with yourself. Understand your purpose, your business plan, and your innovative products and ideas. Then believe in your innovation otherwise you will be destroyed for lack of knowledge. Find the time to have a continuing diligence of self. Keep your resources near you, so you can remain informed in your field of expertise.

Business ethics declares that a client or customer doing transactions with you wants to know the truth. They have great concerns when a misrepresentation or lie surfaces...and it always surfaces. I suggest you never distort the truth. That doesn't mean you must disclose your company secrets. I warn you, a negative perception can destroy your reputation and business. It becomes an affliction that can stop your efforts and potentially kill your business.

I want to prepare you for any possible situation that could happen. So be honest and scholarly. My teachings are not just a hypothetical philosophy. Focus on the advantages of your services and products to your customers or clients. Always remember that an honest relationship is worth more than a few contracts. Your integrity and good name will always be remembered long after your services are over or the use of your product is finished.

I believe that there are possibilities to improve or alter every invention or innovation. Think of your possibilities and your integrity as an assignment for your existence. Find out your calling, purpose, and skills. Pursue them as an Actionaire. Build your life around these self determined assignments. What will your contributions be during your lifetime?

You must activate yourself. Move toward your dreams and ideas. If you are shy, timid, or feel inadequate, you must find the strength within you, to connect with people. It's people who will help you become successful. Those people may not always enable you to succeed. Engage them!

The rules of engagement are simple. There are two types of people, those who already know that you have something they want and those who don't know, at this moment, that you have something they want. Relationships are key to success. It is believed that all people are only 4 degrees apart. In other words, you know Meaghan, who knows Fallon, who knows Michael, who knows Jeanne, combined they will know someone who will know anyone else you would ever want to know. You are therefore networked with the entire community of people.

For you to fulfill your dreams the first things you must do is wake up, then set up, stand up, and speak up. Simply get out of your house and get moving. You will find success somewhere at all times. Begin with the moment and fulfill it. Everyday, when you wake up, you are given 86,400 moments or seconds. That's 24 hours for you math majors. If success begins with someone, then you must go where they are.

Actionaires are accessible people. If you are unwilling to pursue your dreams, you will never possess them. A successful business person doesn't sit in her office and wait for business to show up. They go to their clients and customers. They promote and advertise. They go everywhere and engage dialogue and pitch their products or services. Do you think a banker is going to show up one day at your office and offer you a line of credit? Of course not. What's keeping you from reaching out toward people? Is it a fear of failure, rejection, disappointment, or being turned down? There is one thing distinctly more important to you than being turned down; it's the fulfillment of your dreams, goals, aspirations, and ideas. Living your dream and passion is the crowning jewel in your existence.

People of Action dread rejection, but they are so passionate about their objectives; it's worth the risk. They prepare and research. This gives them the strength to reach beyond their grasp. Now what are your Action items? What are your skills, talents, or innovative ideas? What will you share with someone you trust, that can help you polish your plan and become your mentor? What steps will you take in the next 30 days to develop new business contacts or associates to help your plan? What organizations will you join within the next 45 days that will expand your network of contacts?

Time to Take Action

CHAPTER 1 - PREDICAMENT SOLVING

1. What changes in your lifestyle will you make to find happiness?

___

2. What are the Action items you will engage in to make these changes?

___

3. What attributes do you have that makes you a Predicament Solver?

4. What skillsets do you have that makes you a problem solver?

5. What do you enjoy doing that connects you with your business and lifestyle?

_____
_____
_____
_____
_____
_____
_____
_____
_____

6. What four (4) steps will you take to eliminate the fear of failure?

_____
_____
_____
_____
_____
_____
_____
_____
_____
_____

Action Has No Season 2.0

7. What advantages does your products, goods, and/or services offer your customers?

8. What will you share with someone you trust, that can help you polish your plan and become your mentor?

9. What steps will you take in the next thirty (30) days to develop new business contacts or associates to help your plan?

10. What organizations will you join within the next 45 days that will expand your network of contacts?

11. Define what you want as your legacy.

Chapter 2

TIME MANAGEMENT

Take time to formulate an Action plan. An Actionaire always makes plans, because it is the starting point for any dream or innovation. A plan is a written outline of your arranged Actions. It is necessary to achieve your desired goal. Business associates, clients, and bankers always honor people who plan.

A simple starting point for you is to list things to do every day of your existence. Select 10 items you want to accomplish in your day. Then give total focus and attention to each objective. You should assign a specific time to each item. The lesson I am teaching is if you cannot plan for one day in your life, what gives you the impression you will be successful at accomplishing your goals for a lifetime.

You must consider each moment as a benchmark, and then delegate a specific assignment to each moment. What do you want to accomplish in that time period? Who should you call on? Where should you be networking? Prepare your Action Plan on a written document. If you schedule your activities, your chances of success grow exponentially. This process can be laborious and tedious. This is painstaking, questioning, challenging, and fatiguing. Frankly, it isn't much fun. It is the cost you pay for being the best at what you have chosen to pursue.

Losers avoid planning. They think it's time consuming. What are your primary obstacles in being a more dependable planner? To overcome these obstacles, what will you do in the next 30 days? The secret to leadership and your success is buried in your daily practice. The greatest lessons of life are not taught in a course, which is education imparted through classroom study, but it's on the course of real time experiences.

You plan because there is someone who needs or wants what you are offering. The thought of rejection often gets in the way of taking Action. However, if you experience the challenges of pain, you can foster a lifetime of gain. To succeed, patent your dreams and aspirations, so they will last much longer than a couple of rejections. The Actionaire firmly believes their innovations or inventions are needed by someone. Get past your petrified ego. I apologize, but not everyone will be there to cheer for you. If you determine your goals and dreams are worth the fight, then you will discover your contribution to society will be absolutely necessary for the success of others, as well as yourself.

Hank Aaron was the greatest home run hitter for many years. He was truly the home run king of baseball. Most people never considered the fact that he had more strike outs than he had home runs. We don't remember his losses at bat. We primarily just recall his successes. He had the courage to step into that batter's box and risk the possibility of a strike out in order to hit a home run. He took risks to achieve his goal. You must learn to step into the batter's box of the business world. This is a daily requirement to have courage and embrace your passion.

Most great capitalists say, knowing that 9 out of 10 will turn you down, is nothing more than inspiration and to hustle through as many people as possible to find that one who will buy. Learning to handle rejection is a secret to success. To the Actionaire, "No." merely means ask again.

You don't have to close on every project, idea, or sale in order to succeed. If you plant your seeds, you will enjoy a harvest. You can plant your seeds of knowledge and change someone.

You have many purposes and one of them is to change others. Literally every person you meet is trying to change in some way. They strive for excellence and financial freedom. They desire good mental and physical health to stay strong. Happiness is wished for and loneliness is rejected. Your purpose is to help someone through your innovative thinking and Action. Your business ideas may not qualify to help every person, but it might be the type of innovative ideas that could change their life someday.

Most people want a change in their life; however, they don't know how to manage their time. People want to succeed and improve. You must have something others need and it will change their life. They have been waiting for a lifetime for you to pursue your possibilities. It is up to you to manage your time and find that product, item, or idea that will help people change. This means business for you. It means expanding your purpose to be creative and innovative.

What is your core expertise? Whatever your gift is, take Action on it. It is something others need and will pay richly to obtain.

Time to Take Action

CHAPTER 2 – TIME MANAGEMENT

1. Formulate and outline your Action Plan with timetables.

___

2. What new business challenges do you want to accomplish within the next 30 days?

___

3. Who will you call on for guidance?

_____
_____
_____
_____
_____
_____
_____
_____
_____

4. What events will you attend to network with other Actionaires?

_____
_____
_____
_____
_____
_____
_____
_____
_____
_____
_____

5. What are your primary obstacles in becoming a more dependable planner?

_____

_____

_____

_____

_____

_____

_____

_____

_____

6. How would you define your top five (5) skills that you can apply in your business?

_____

_____

_____

_____

_____

_____

_____

_____

_____

Chapter 3

BELIEVE IN YOURSELF

Doesn't it seem as if everyone has an opinion of you? They want to change you in one way or another. The reality is nobody truly knows you. Think of this for a second or two. Isn't it true that nearly everyone in your life is more focused on themselves rather than you? Always remember this; you know more about yourself than anyone you will ever meet.

The Actionaires are never concerned with what others say, it is what you believe regarding yourself that matters. You may be falsely accused, slandered, and have negative rumors hurled at you, but it should never affect you. I want you to be happy because your reward is great. You must fulfill your plan. Believe in yourself. Only you know what you are really about. Trust in your innovation skills and your business ideas. People always go against what they don't comprehend.

Your naysayers, critics, haters, and backstabbers are ignorant, unschooled and egotistical. History is a witness that Actionaires have had their names trashed and stained. Even some of the greatest innovators and inventors have been slandered. Great civil rights leaders, ministers, and political leaders have as well.

Thomas Edison tried a thousand times to invent the light bulb.

He was shunned and was the butt of many jokes. But once the press conference was called to demonstrate his invention, the press core asked, "What do you have to say to your critics now?" He didn't speak a word. He just walked over to the light bulb, turned it on and walked away. Edison was an Actionaire. He never begged anyone to believe in him. He knew that integrity would prevail. His focus on his dream, vision, and aspiration would win in the end.

You should never waste time with critics. Keep your attention on your goal. Stay focused. You should never strive to appear confident, be confident. Don't struggle to have character, be of good character and reputation. When you start your business, don't ask the question, can this business work? Speak in the affirmative, this business will work!

The Actionaire wants people to admire and respect them, but the fact is your enemies and critics will never leave your good status unsoiled and unblemished. You must rise above that fact. You must never allow what others say about you change your personal opinion of yourself. Period...never.

What is your reward for staying the course? For a capitalist the reward is money! When you succeed in your business, you will have a reward day; commonly called a *payday*. You are rewarded for spending your best moments of each day. Your vigor and comprehension is focused on building your specific goals, and for this, you get paid.

Money is very important to every capitalist. You cannot live without it. You cannot provide for your family or assist your community without it. Try going into a clothing store, car dealership, or checking into a hotel without it. Money is a fact of life. It is a necessity. Acting on your dreams and goals, brings you closer to being prosperous and living an abundant life. Your future rests in your mind within the moment. Nothing is too tiny to multiply and grow. Being productive is possible by everyone. It includes sharing knowledge and offering assistance.

In business, if I give you a dollar and you give me a dollar, we both only end up with a dollar. But if I give you an idea and you give me an idea, now we both have two ideas.

The Actionaire takes the time to show their associates how to make money. By planting a seed with someone, you could reap a harvest. Achieving financial freedom is the way to go. Focus your mind on the true source of capitalism. Selling your products or services to someone is helping them while helping yourself. Winning in business helps everyone. Sowing your seeds of help, will lead to a financial harvest.

Time to Take Action

CHAPTER 3 – BELIEVE IN YOURSELF

1. How will you focus on your business plans while avoiding the distractions of others?

2. Write down five (5) affirmations that will be your focus on a daily basis that you believe in and will encourage you everyday.

3. How will you reward yourself for staying the course of believing in yourself?

4. What are your skill sets that influence others and how will you plant your seeds of knowledge?

Chapter 4

INNER CITY INNOVATION CENTERS

In September 2010, I attended the inaugural meeting of the National Advisory Council on Innovation and Entrepreneurship. This is considered a prestigious appointment by the Secretary of Commerce, Gary Lott. We were tasked to provide advice to President Barack Obama's Administration on ways to identify, inspire, and assist business innovation and entrepreneurialism.

We wanted manufacturing opportunities to be insourced versus outsourced. As I sat in this first meeting held in the boardroom of the Secretary of Commerce, I heard from representatives from the Commerce Department, the Small Business Administration, and the White House, I knew one of the first challenges to get the United States back on its feet, was by having more products manufactured in the United States.

It was commonly believed that, that would happen through innovation. To define it in a way that is not normally viewed. As I sat next to Steve Case, the founder of AOL, we listened to the presidents of Michigan University and Georgia Tech, representatives from MIT, Carnegie Mellon University, and Howard University. They sang a similar tone. The Government should fund laboratories for the innovator on their school grounds. Although, that was one solution,

I proposed the creation of the Urban Center for Innovation and Entrepreneurship. I proposed these centers to be placed in the inner city communities where locals of all ages can come and be creative and help achieve the desired results of the President's administration.

I question this assumption as it appears. To me, we need a driver for creativity. Consider yourself a creative person and you can turn it on like you would the air conditioning system in your house. You cool off, become relaxed, and maybe take a nap, in the cool air on a hot summer's day. You then turn it off until you need it again. On those days you could accomplish anything.

However, we all had those days, when the cooling system didn't work. The filters needed changing and the compressor was out of service. It's hot outside and inside. Nothing seems to come together. You can't just sit around and wait for inspiration to hit. Beginners, in the world of innovation, sometimes wait for inspiration. The real innovators get up and take Action every day. They understand that you are not born with creativity, and you have to cultivate creativity in an ongoing way.

The Actionaire innovator keeps a common place book of ideas as soon as they come to them. They keep a journal near them at all times. A hand written paper manual or on their iPad. It offers you the opportunity to make sketches and drawings, however, any way you can capture your thought will serve the purpose. When you need to fire up your creativity, search your manual for ideas and examples.

A professional innovator questions everything, asking the "Why?", "How?", and "Who?" questions in order to determine if there is a better way to a solution. "What's missing?" is a popular question. To find inspiration, an innovator, searches the surrounding environment. Sculptors find inspiration in many unexpected places. If looking at the same four walls of a laboratory, your perspective will always be limited.

Time to Take Action

CHAPTER 4 – INNER CITY INNOVATION CENTERS

1. What will you do to inspire your creativity?

_____
_____
_____
_____
_____
_____
_____
_____
_____

2. How will you tap into your creativity?

_____
_____
_____
_____
_____
_____
_____
_____
_____

3. What talents come easily and effortlessly to you?

_____
_____
_____
_____
_____
_____
_____
_____
_____

4. What attributes do you possess that people compliment you on?

_____
_____
_____
_____
_____
_____
_____
_____
_____

5. Identify five (5) creative ideas that will allow you to start your business or expand it.

6. Where will you go to find inspiration to spark your creativity?

Chapter 5

INSPIRATION TO ACT

What inspires people to act? People are motivated by two forms of stimulus: loss or gain, hurt or pleasure, terror or prize. When you ask your child to clean their room, they might complain and make the argument that they don't feel like it. They would rather play video games with their friends. Now you have two ways to inspire this child; loss or gain, hurt or pleasure, terror or prize.

An example would be to tell this child to bring you a stick from outside, then bend over, and prepare to be disciplined. Or, you could use a reward method. You would say to your child, if you clean up your room I will pay your allowance in advance and allow you to live. That's a joke, but you parents know what I'm talking about. The advance payment on the allowance is a reward, gain, or prize. In the business world we reward those who help us succeed.

The Actionaire is created with a burning desire to increase. Decreasing is unnatural. I believe that every person you encounter in life wants to increase. They want to be rewarded for their efforts. This is a positive thing. It is a natural act of nature to do more and multiply. However, be careful to research the benefits you offer to those helping you and your business. If you are selling a product, who needs it, why do they want it, and is it something they can find elsewhere?

Examine the incentives of your company. Know them well. This will be important both with your customers and your employees. People buy your products, goods and services, and employees work more diligently. They know what the prize is for them at the end of the day.

The Actionaire motivates and inspires people through incentives. People do things for different reasons. I suggest you meet and interview them. By asking questions you can learn what their strongest needs are and in so doing, you might discover their deepest fears.

An Actionaire solves problems and challenges. Always take time to educate others on the value of your proposition for them. Make sure they understand the importance of working for you or doing business with you. The rewards and benefits are clearly expressed and committed. Outside of a pay check, how do you inspire those who helped you succeed?

Inspiring people through financial rewards may not be the only or best way to motivate them into performing. Someone may prefer to be mentored. They may view that as a way to grow. The Actionaire is also a teacher. It has been said that you don't learn anything when you talk: you only learn when you listen. I believe that is true. You might observe some of the greatest thoughts and ideas after you have lectured or given a speech.

One of the reasons I wrote this book was to mentor through the written word. A mentor helps you get down the road of success faster. Teaching is extremely important. The Actionaire teaches. You should share what you have learned. This is especially true for your employees, fellow businesspersons, and children, in which you are in contact with or have governance over. Successful capitalists have employees who are informed, well trained, and confident about carrying out their instruction. This takes time to accomplish, along with energy and patience.

No human was born with imperial knowledge. Instinct yes, knowledge no. We become who or what we are. We discover what we have learned. This learning takes hours, focus, and fortitude. A capitalist must invest time into cultivating their vision, their product data, and the return you want for it. Developing your human intellectual capital requires the same or greater effort as your personal training. You must have good people around you. The Actionaire inspires those people. Frequently, in their life, you are the primary mentor.

You must educate your staff. Constantly motivate them. Show leadership that offers a future for their commitment. This also builds succession within your business. There is no success without succession.

Time to Take Action

CHAPTER 5 – INSPIRATION TO ACT

1. What inspires you to take action in your everyday life?

_____
_____
_____
_____
_____
_____
_____
_____
_____
_____

2. What inspires you to take action in your business?

_____
_____
_____
_____
_____
_____
_____
_____
_____
_____

3. If you are considering going into business, ask yourself the following questions:

a. Who is your target market?

_____
_____
_____
_____
_____
_____
_____
_____
_____

b. How will you approach your target market?

_____
_____
_____
_____
_____
_____
_____
_____
_____

c. What are you selling?

d. Why do prospective clients need or want what you have to offer?

e. Is it something they can find elsewhere?

_____
_____
_____
_____
_____
_____
_____
_____

f. How will you make your price point competitive?

_____
_____
_____
_____
_____
_____
_____
_____

4. What are the incentives or benefits for someone who does business with you?

5. Write down three (3) – five (5) questions to ask your clients to learn their greatest needs.

6. What do you do to inspire others?

_____
_____
_____
_____
_____
_____
_____
_____
_____

7. List five (5) of your characteristics that can inspire others.

_____
_____
_____
_____
_____
_____
_____
_____
_____
_____

Chapter 6

AN ACHIEVER'S MINDSET

The mindset is defined as an established set of attitudes held by someone.

A mindset is taught. Approximately 79 percent of Americans live pay check to pay check, and 69 percent of people in business break even or lose money. Most people in America don't have any disposable income, unfortunately they have accepted the fact that they don't have any currency to save. They overspend or spend beyond their financial capacity. They don't know how to make or multiply what money they have. In their minds, they are constantly fearful of having a lack of cash. It is said that America is "The land of the free and the home of the brave", but that is not even close to the truth.

Usually, poor people say, "I don't know how to make money" or they don't take the time to create an income. They use this as an excuse, while complaining about not having enough funds. Complaining has no value. If you complain about not having enough money, work more. If you complain about not enjoying your life, take a vacation. The Actionaire takes action to make changes in their life. Don't just sit there and complain. Let your actions dictate a new direction. It's just that easy. Don't stand in one place like you don't have control. Do you need to take a walk in the park? Don't say you don't have the time. That's just an excuse, it's an escape. Don't be lazy, take a walk in the park especially when, in fact, you really can take that walk. Position your mindset to take action and stop procrastinating.

If you want real value in your life, take on the position that money alone doesn't have value. Rather it's the personal and real property you can buy, or the goods and services you acquired with it. Most people don't understand that money is a vector for expressing value. It's a tool to get value. Value is in the labor you put into earning the money, which then assists you in acquiring that which you value. It's your mindset that elevates you from poverty to riches.

Poverty is passed on and taught, most frequently by exposed behavior, in your family. A middle-class lifestyle is learned at home, school, and church. Building wealth is instructed and emulated within the society, business, and professional world experienced within the environment inhabited by you and your colleagues. Those poor, and in some cases, middle-class people are constantly struggling and always worried about money. This demonstrates a mindset that was probably showing up in their family or the people who influenced them.

You can escape from this mindset. Far too many people are trapped in a situation like a boring job and they feel like there is no hope or future for them. They come to their job everyday depressed and feeling locked down. They feel like there is no light at the end of the tunnel, no rainbow with a pot of gold for them. They suffer through a 9 to 5 daily job only because they were taught to go to school, get a job with benefits, and retire with a basic pension. That alone can be incredibly limiting.

The Actionaire has dreams or ideas to pursue. To achieve them, their mindset dictates that they must set aside some hours in the day to develop and pursue those business ideas. This is very possible for you. Just free those ideas. While growing up you may not have been encouraged to take risks and go into business. Face it, most people don't take chances so they look for a safe job. A job that lets you pay your credit cards and buy or lease a car and a home. These are the items that keep you in debt and trapped to that safe but boring job.

It might be safe, but are you happy? How do you get out?

It was once said, "a person who does not enjoy the fruits of their labor is nothing more than a modern day slave."

You must plan your break out. Set aside some money to escape. Realize you are required to have discipline. You have to go for it. If you are stuck in that job and are a modern day slave, you must find a way to cut that golden handcuffs. Felicity is addictive. You will need to be prepared to make a highly risky move to get out. Your happiness is worth it. You jump in the water when you want to learn to swim, but you might drown. What I mean is, if you don't jump into the ocean of business opportunities you may miss your contentment. Why don't people go for it? The main reason one doesn't break free from that boring comfort zone is because they value other people's opinions of them as having the status of a "good" job, rather than being happy.

The Actionaire has a free mindset. When people say the sky is the limit, she remembers that there is more because there are footprints on the moon.

A great mind is an achieving mind. To meet this standard your mindset must be persistent, persevering, assertive, and fearless.

It's your mindset that creates your destiny.

Words are powerful and certain words pass between people offering pleasantries during a farewell moment. Phrases like, "Have a nice day," or the shorter version, "Have a nice one." Though well intentioned it was never clear as to exactly what it means. So, I came up with a farewell message for the Actionaire. This one offers a true direction to encourage action. Let's accept this farewell message and pass it on to our friends, family, and fellow Actionaires.

Simply say, "HAVE AN ACHIEVING DAY!"

Time to Take Action

CHAPTER 6 – AN ACHIEVER'S MINDSET

1. How are you spending the necessary time to expand your thoughts?

___

2. How much time do you spend cultivating an awareness of your possibilities?

___

3. State these possibilities and how many hours, per day, do you invest in becoming informed of these possibilities?

_____
_____
_____
_____
_____
_____
_____
_____
_____

4. Define your calling, purpose, and skills in the world of business.

_____
_____
_____
_____
_____
_____
_____
_____
_____

5. What are your skills, talents, or innovative ideas?

6. What will you do to help develop your mindset to reach your goals?

Chapter 7

ATTITUDE CONTROL

The essential occurrence of the Actionaire is to not be resentful over your business disappointments. Think, you can design the perfect business plan, but you can't predict the perfect economic conditions, so learn to discard the past and recognize that everyday won't be profitable. If and when you find yourself misplaced in the shadow of desperation, remember: it's only at night that you see the north star, and that star will lead you home and back in focus.

The Actionaire isn't afraid to make mistakes, to stumble and fall; because most of the times, the greatest victory may come from doing things that frighten you the greatest. There is a time in life when you step away from all the dramatic individuals who create a negative environment. The Actionaire surrounds themselves with people who contribute to their happiness, they forget the negative, and focus on the positive things in life.

As an Actionaire, embrace the people who treat you right, and offer best wishes for the ones who don't. Respond to your heart and follow your dreams; move forward notwithstanding those things that are inevitable to change. The life of your business is like life itself, too short to be anything but enjoyable and prosperous. Don't let it be controlled by the will of others, which could cause you pain.

However, as life will have it, in the end, some of your greatest pains, might turn into some of your greatest strengths.

An Actionaire sees life clearly and realizes that falling down is a part of life. However, the true strength and character of a business and a person is getting back up. Then it is living life to its fullest and remembering to enjoy yourself on the way. You may not get everything you planned, or you may end up with more than you ever imagined. The unconventional truth is that no one knows where life can take you or your business.

In short, when in business you will experience a downturn. Try not to count what you lost, rather hold what you possess with affection. Formulate a new plan and take Action to achieve it, because the past will never return, but the future may compensate for those losses and propel your business into greater and more prosperous profits.

For the Actionaire, attitude and choices are the core of life's structure. In many ways life is a "Do-It-Yourself Kit". You build your business like a contractor builds a building, one nail and one board at a time. It is your attitude and choices that help you build for your life tomorrow. It is therefore important for you to not build foolishly.

Remember, you cannot go back and start a new beginning. You can, however, start today and make a new ending. The Actionaire's life is a matter of perspective and always relative. You can either complain that the sun is too hot or you can celebrate that you are alive to feel its warmth. It all depends on your perspective. In the business world you must learn to hold your peace. When on the surface of a transaction there seems to be disruption, the Actionaire knows that the core on the deal is steady, it is critical to hold your peace, and stay calm. When I look at the ocean during a storm I see the waves may be rough on top, but I know that deeper in the sea there is calm. Don't conduct your business or live on the surface, live beneath the violent waves, and seek out the deep waters. Don't be moved by those aggressive waves.

Those waves will frustrate and distract you. Life is too short. Nothing should frustrate you. Wear your clothing of peace when you leave your house and enter your place of business. When you endure those distractions without flinching or canceling a deal out of mere frustration...everything will be fine. Stay at rest, at peace because you may not know what the future may bring, but we know there will be a future and keeping your eye on the prize and avoid the misdirection that might be thrown in your path. Handle your situation with confidence and prepare for the future without fear. Don't believe your distractors and don't question your beliefs. Being an Actionaire is wonderful if you know how to live.

The Actionaire will not apologize for the life that they have lived. They won't regret the experiences that they had, nor will they fear the future that they are hoping to have because they know that everything that is challenging gives them courage to be better than they are and over time, they will grow.

The reality of life clears matters and creates the expectations of change and challenges. The Actionaire knows from experience that they will not always be victorious. Frankly, the greater win is accepting your short-fall and weaknesses and giving respect to the other party. Low points exist in everyone's life. What defines an Actionaire is the way they pick themselves up after being knocked down. Therefore, you must always embrace the moment.

Where you are right now? Why, because nothing in your lifetime will last forever, whether it is happiness or sadness. If you are on a beautiful sunny Caribbean beach, rejoice, because the night will come and the sun will disappear. If it is at night when you're on the beach, enjoy the stars and the moon with the understanding that the clouds will come and change the view. When in business, there are times when you will walk the trails of disappointment and tribulations but the Actionaire knows that the little pain they went through was nothing compared to the life fulfillment and joy of living their dream and succeeding in business. Those so called bad things in life or business can open your eyes to the good things you weren't noticing before.

The Actionaire sees their business dream as something you have to give everything to achieve. But they never let their successes go to their head or their disappointments go to their heart. They believe that when they have a good attitude, they can control everything in their life no matter what it is.

Stay in an attitude of faith. Stay in an attitude of hope. If you think you are in an unfair situation, the banks won't make a loan, you can't reach the level of sales you need; if you become bitter, you will create regret, a negative stimulus or grief. Refuse to let your life be bitter. Develop your business with a mindset of hope. Let your dream take root inside your thoughts of hope, belief, and high expectations. A habit of hope produces a habit of Action. If you don't contemplate a future, you will not have a present.

Your business today consists of those yesterday choices.

Time to Take Action

CHAPTER 7 – ATTITUDE CONTROL

1. **Name the three (3) most influential people in your life and explain their influence over you.**

2. **Why do you consider these people to be a positive influence in your life?**

3. List five (5) positive experiences in your life that make you who you are.

4. What made these experiences positive for you?

5. What techniques do you implement to find peace and relaxation in your life and business?

6. How will you maintain hope in your business and lifestyle while staying faithful to your beliefs?

Chapter 8

LIFE'S TRANSFORMATIONS

It is said that a cat has nine lives. I don't know if that is true, but I know they always land on their feet. The Actionaire Exam relates to that statement. They always land on their feet.

Life takes us through transformations. This comes about when you change the food, the information and the education you feed yourself. Much like a caterpillar that lives in a cocoon surviving on the same food within the cocoon, you must transition into a butterfly to break out. This transformation is introduced in the magnificence of its potential by forming a butterfly. Its colors of wings, the delicacies of its stature and its ability to find fresh nutritious food, demonstrate nature's remarkable ability to foster the survival of a living being. Do you want to fly like a butterfly or would your rather keep crawling like a caterpillar?

Transformation of the food you consume, or metaphorically, the people you are associated with, helps you take the new course of Action. You must change where you are going and not continue to stay the course of where you've been. You can change externally easily, but to change internally you feed yourself with what you want to change into. If you said everything in your thoughts, you might not be who you want to be, so you have learned to control your utterances. There is always a struggle between your mind and your mouth. If you want to do something different, you must pass the Actionaire Exam.

Change the feedings connected to your thoughts and you will change where you are going. You will always be directed via thinking; if you change your thinking you will change your direction.

Nothing is ever permanent and a transition will occur if you are an Actionaire.

Don't believe the *"never"* lies.

It's *never* going to happen for me.

It's *never* going to work.

I will *never* be out of debt.

My business will *never succeed.*

They will *never* like me.

I will *never* get well.

My life will *never* change.

If you feed yourself with the belief you can transition your life, it will occur.

Keep your hopes up, become a believer and not a doubter. Your life is shifting for you. This will be an exceptional time for you. Take Action, be encouraged, step away from fear, and the *"never"* lies.

There is a story about a man who opened his lunch and pulled out a baloney sandwich. Looking at his friend he says, "I hate baloney!", his friend comments by asking why doesn't he tell his wife to prepare something other than baloney. The man responded by indicating he was not married and that he prepares his own lunch. The lesson is that sometimes we pack into our life a lot of baloney.

Plato once said, "Human nature is like a two-headed strong horse pulling in opposite directions."

The Actionaire understands that within us there is a little bad in the best of us and a little good in the worst of us. Your business, your family, and you are great because you are good, if you cease to be good you will cease to be great.

Your transformation can come at any age. I have heard of someone who died at 55 years old but wasn't buried until they were 95. Becoming an Actionaire brings life back to you. I heard people speaking of retiring, to me that term should be "re-tiring" or putting on new tires for the fun and challenging journey in your future. You have seeds of greatness in you. Get that ambition back and go for those dreams. It's not over as long as you embrace a transition and change.

This is the time for you to create a business breakthrough. Don't focus on what you don't have, rather, focus on what you have and where you want to go. Your season is now, but you have to catch the wind. The young locusts have very small wings and they struggle while learning to fly. However, their destiny to fly occurs when their instinct takes control and it tells them to wait for the right wind to blow, and then leap. That leap lifts the locust into the wind which supports its desire to take flight. The Actionaire takes flight in business through instinct. They take that leap of faith, and then fly. The Actionaire understands this concept of a leap of faith.

Your transition will require a leap of faith. When you get that destiny call, you will feel the leap within you. You fit into life when you pursue your purpose and become great at what you do. Progress has a process. We all have seasons and we must go through phases in our life.

The transition occurs with your change of appetite. The Actionaire feeds on positive thinking and avoids the negative. There are so many negative elements invading our thoughts from television news, talk radio, songs, and people. Your environment is full of dead food and negative images.

What's feeding you? You become what you consume. The buzzard eats of the dead, the eagle soars high because it feeds off live food. We are not trash cans. Be an eagle. Fill yourself with live food and positive thoughts. Listen to those who help you think and act positive. Make a positive contribution with your life, that's how you fit in society.

Time to Take Action

CHAPTER 8 – LIFE'S TRANSFORMATIONS

1. How will you break free from psychological restrictions that have you trapped in a virtual cocoon?

___

2. What will you do to enhance your growth and transformation?

___

3. What actions will you take to pursue your dreams?

_____
_____
_____
_____
_____
_____
_____
_____
_____
_____

Chapter 9

REPOSITIONING YOURSELF

This story is about a basketball game when I hurt myself after turning my ankle. For the balance of the game I was limping. That injury affected every part of my body because anything that creates a shift causes change.

Change hurts sometimes. When you experience a change you have to understand that it is time for repositioning. When you are stagnant and stuck, you have to also reposition. Don't look for a miracle to correct your situation; you create the miracle for yourself and for someone else. The Actionaire's instinct dictates they must reposition their life or their business to bring it into alignment. Instinct is the evidence of the things not seen but felt.

If you are struggling between what you are and what you want to be in life, you need to reposition. Often people have a fear of running out of time. This causes anxiety, concerns, and stress. Like the basketball injury, if you don't act on it, a stiffing will take over and cause a debilitating situation. You will feel out of sync. To come into alignment, you must be open to a realignment and a repositioning.

There are times when the wind seems to blow against you. The Actionaire takes a positive view through the analogy that a plane takes off with the wind blowing against it. It is those winds in the face of the plane that creates the lift. When an eagle faces hard blowing winds or a harsh storm, the eagle simply opens its wings and lets the wind lift it higher until it rises above the storm until it finds a calmer place. This can be achieved by changing your mental position.

So many people have a self-imposed timidity about them. You were not born with timidity. To be an Actionaire you must divorce yourself from timidity. Timidity is a magnifier of fear. Fear is the base of most of our problems. This causes you to stop inwardly. Fear then places you in bondage. It will paralyze you. Don't live in fear, step out and be bold; come out of your comfort zone. I want you to wake up believing you can do whatever you want to do. If you have fear, you can't achieve.

When you take the steps necessary to plan your business, you must have a sober mind. Fear makes you drunk and you can not pass a sobriety test when your mind is impaired. Your fear is so imposing you cannot walk a straight line. Sobriety requires discipline.

The Actionaire is a disciplined businessperson. When it is time to handle their business issues, they set their face like a stone sculpture, they stay focused. They don't look to the left or the right, fear is never a factor. They live to please themselves and not someone else. They ignore negative people, the envious, the jealous, and especially those small minded people. Never argue with small minded individuals over insignificant issues. The Actionaire, however, remains kind and considerate but dusts off unimportant remarks. You must live to please yourself and always be yourself.

If you are going to reposition yourself, you must attain new levels of engagement. Your best is not behind you, it is ahead of you. The Actionaire is always in a state of elevation and growth.

I am reminded of a story of a man fishing next to a friend of his and he was doing a great job of catching all sizes of fish. But, what the friend noticed was he only kept the small ones and threw back the large ones. He had to ask, "Why are you only keeping the small ones and tossing back the large fish?" The man catching all the fish said, "It is because I only have a 10-inch frying pan!"

Do you have what I refer to as a 10-inch frying pan mentality? Do you always only expect to live with the small things in life? Get rid of the 10-inch frying pan mentality! Who says you can't get a bigger house, a better car, or build a global company? Are you bold enough to say I can and will start a business?

All you need to do is enlarge your vision. Believe in something bigger and better for you. When you do that, you will change and fear and timidity will disappear. Don't get discouraged, believe in an explosive blessing. You are heavy with big dreams and that will lead you to accomplishing your destiny.

Life chose what you are and who you are; but you choose how you go through life.

I don't want to dictate to you, I just want to talk to you.

Now be an Actionaire, go out, and buy a bigger frying pan!

Time to Take Action

CHAPTER 9 – REPOSITIONING YOURSELF

1. **What are the areas in your life that you need to reposition?**

   _____
   _____
   _____
   _____
   _____
   _____
   _____
   _____
   _____

2. **Where will you go to find new information to help you during the process of your repositioning?**

   _____
   _____
   _____
   _____
   _____
   _____
   _____
   _____
   _____

Action Has No Season 2.0

3. How will you allow your instincts to serve as your internal compass to guide you?

___

Chapter 10

LIVE WITH EXPECTANCY

The Actionaire believes in oneself. When you begin to believe in yourself you will birth a change in your life. In 2015, two of my daughters were pregnant. It was exciting for the family and those around us knowing two new lives were soon to join us. Live with great potential. The mothers felt expectancy within them. A change that will make their lives different, challenging, and exciting.

Much like giving birth to a child, you must understand birthing your potential requires some pain and discomfort.

Let's equate beginning your business and becoming a true Actionaire to being pregnant.

When you are pregnant with a business idea, that conception brings ideas, excitement, and expectations.

You must understand that this brings change in your life. This change will require you to believe in yourself. It is only then will you bring forth or birth your potential.

Too frequently one looks outside for direction and guidance. The Actionaire begins by looking inside to draw confidence and vision. Believing in your expectancy and feeling your passion leads to the delivery of the potential. You should live everyday with your expectancy and not with that which others tell you to expect.

When starting a business times can be tough, uncomfortable, and painful. However, those are signs of birth delivery. In those times you must remember that they are the equivalent of labor pains.

The banks are not cooperating, your office leasing is too expensive, staff member are not sharing your vision, doors are closed in your face, and you feel rejection…labor pains. Just do your part; and success will follow. You will give birth to your vision.

As an Actionaire, your business vision and passion feels like something is kicking inside of you. Although you cannot see it, you feel it, and you know it is inside and will come to life. You have already conceived your business plan. You are pregnant with success and talent. Don't talk yourself out of delivering your dream. Don't abort your seeds of greatness. Don't become victims of your environment…rather become victors!

Feel that business kicking inside of you. You may be the only one to see it or feel it but remember you are carrying the seed of your destiny. A destiny only you can create. It is inside you.

The change in your life will come when you believe in yourself and give birth to your potential.

Time to Take Action

CHAPTER 10 – LIVE WITH EXPECTANCY

1. Why do you believe in yourself?

_____
_____
_____
_____
_____
_____
_____
_____
_____

2. What will you do each day to affirm your belief in yourself?

_____
_____
_____
_____
_____
_____
_____
_____
_____

3. How will you prepare for the birth of your new business or growth of your current business?

_____
_____
_____
_____
_____
_____
_____
_____
_____
_____

4. List 3 things you can do to prepare for the birthing of your potential.

_____
_____
_____
_____
_____
_____
_____
_____
_____
_____

Chapter 11

GET ON THE RIGHT TRACK

If you were to say to yourself, "I am comfortable defining myself as an employee or a job holder," it might be very difficult to see yourself as an entrepreneur or a capitalist searching to become a multi-millionaire. It is generally because your mind has placed you in a pattern that would make this difficult to relate to existing outside for the comfort and security of a job.

When I was in elementary school the St. Louis Public Schools required all graduating students to take a test to determine one's projected level of competence for high school learning. This was called the Tracking System. When a student took the exam, they would be classified as track 1A, 1, 2, or 3. At that very point in life, as a graduating 8th grader, you would be tested to see how smart you were, which ultimately directed you to limit or define you for the rest of your life.

As I recall my view of things. I was confused as to why some who I felt were bright and capable tested in the lower tracks. Just this one test could, place some of these young students in a mindset of inferiority. Unfortunately, they stayed in the lower mindset of a person who was not suppose to achieve great heights. If you see yourself as a "C" student, then "Cs" will come to you and you will rationalize that grade as the best you can do. If you call upon a negative or inferior existence, you will more than likely live that way.

There once was a man who was told he could only be a construction laborer. One day the company he worked for closed and he was out of a job. When applying for a new job he was required to take an intelligence quota test. His scores were in the top 5%. He later started his own business, patented several items and became wildly successful.

The track that he was originally placed on was far from the true person. Once he learned how profoundly smart he was, he became an Actionaire. He placed new positive thoughts in his mind which lead to a bright new lifestyle.

You are an amazing masterpiece. There will not be another one of you. You are to never down yourself or let anyone or any backwards school system down you. Don't ever see yourself as a failure, not good enough, or a non-achiever. They might say you just don't measure up or you are washed up. Change all those words, those negative impressions. You are a superior being and you were born perfect. Never say you are weak, inferior, unqualified when in fact you are strong and equipped to fulfill your dreams and business plans.

What someone says about you does not determine your destiny. The Actionaire always looks forward, knowing that he or she are one of a kind, secure, remarkably talented, and triumphant. You have incredible and untapped potential. First you must change inside. Never, ever, be against yourself. You have talents and gifts that are unique to only you. Don't ever think you are inferior, unqualified, or incompetent. Those thoughts create fear and resistance.

To be an Actionaire you must be insanely optimistic. Not only do you see the glass as half full, you know there are more full glasses in the cabinet.

Use words and thoughts that elevate you. Use words that bring positive thoughts of your future and not words that bring you down. By birth, you are approved and accepted. You have seeds of greatness. Change your mindset. Tell yourself you are beautiful, handsome, smart, and that you get things done. Know who and what you are and not what someone has told you what or who you are.

Time to Take Action

CHAPTER 11 – GET ON THE RIGHT TRACK

1. **What are some of the negative beliefs that you are still holding onto because of what someone said to you or about you?**

   _____
   _____
   _____
   _____
   _____
   _____
   _____
   _____
   _____
   _____

2. **How will you take Action to begin the process of letting go of these negative beliefs?**

   _____
   _____
   _____
   _____
   _____
   _____
   _____
   _____
   _____

3. Write down your dreams, goals, vision, and business plan.

_____
_____
_____
_____
_____
_____
_____
_____
_____

4. How frequently will you review these plans as you continue to grow in your everyday life and business?

_____
_____
_____
_____
_____
_____
_____
_____
_____

5. What will be your five (5) affirmations that you will follow consistently over the next thirty (30) days that will keep you on track?

_____
_____
_____
_____
_____
_____
_____
_____
_____
_____

Chapter 12

BUILD YOUR OWN FENCE

The Actionaire will not apologize for the life that they live, won't regret the experiences that they've had, nor will they fear the future that they're hoping to have because they know that everything they are not, gives them courage to be better than they are and over time, people grow; things get clear and expectations change. An Actionaire has learned that they don't always have to win. Sometimes, the greater prize is accepting their weaknesses and disappointments and giving the respect to someone else.

Everyone has low points in their life. What defines us, is the way we choose to adjust ourselves and recover. So, never forget to enjoy the moment where you are right NOW, because nothing lasts forever, whether it's good or bad. If it's a valley REJOICE, because your mountain is up ahead. If you're on the mountain, EMBRACE it with an understanding that seasons change. After becoming an Actionaire you will walk through your trials and tribulations. You will notice that the pain you went through was nothing compared to the joy you will experience with your ultimate success.

When you are moving into a positive state of business development, there will be those who are envious and will criticize you and your business. These are negative people who want you to fail to make them feel more positive about themselves. They will never support you no matter what you do to win them over. It's never enough regardless of how you try. The Actionaire builds their own protection fence and keeps their fence up against people like this.

Your life has both vertical and horizontal elements. The closer you get to becoming successful vertically, the more you will have horizontal attacks by people who only mean you harm or make attempts to cause you grief, despair, and confusion. No matter what you say or do, they have something negative against you. These people you must ignore or keep your fence up against them.

Someone once said, 25% of the people will never like you regardless of what you do. Another 25% may not like you but can be persuaded to like you. The next 25% like you but could be persuaded not to like you. The last 25% cares for you and will always be in you corner no matter what.

In October 2010 the Omni Hotel Group closed their Detroit Hotel. This hotel was located on the Detroit Riverwalk. This location offered views of the Detroit River, the beautiful Belle Isle and Windsor Canada. This is a fabulous 108 room hotel with great potential. It was in disrepair but remained operational. The physical grounds were once occupied by the Park-Davis Pharmaceutical Company. The hotel was occupied as an office and animal laboratory. I heard stories of various animals such as horses and monkeys populating the grounds and monkeys escaping and hiding in the ceiling rafters. They said on any given day pregnant women would line up on McDougal Street to sell their urine for research.

Eventually the greater Park-Davis Pharmaceutical Complex was purchased by the Stroh Family known for its beer and ice cream. Their family company then began to convert the properties into a mixed use development comprising offices, apartments, condominiums, parking garages, and hotel. The laboratory building was completely transformed into a hotel and opened in 1989. The cost was over $18 million. Shortly after the Stroh's opened the hotel they lost it due to a failure to properly manage the construction costs. After changing ownership a couple of times, the Omni Hotel company stepped in and purchased the property. They held on for eleven years. As a result of the economy's 2008 crash and the downfall of the City of Detroit due to the failure of the automobile industry and years of political corruption, Omni turned their backs on Detroit and left. The hotel was closed and boarded up.

I was called months in advance to the closing to visit the Omni Hotel in Detroit by their regional manager. He was an old friend whom assisted me in the purchase of my first hotel eight years earlier when he was with Wyndham hotels. Given the size and location of the hotel, he thought I should consider adding it to our now 14 hotel group.

Agreeing to check it out, I took a quick trip to Detroit. I was warned by many to avoid investing in that city. They stated Detroit was corrupt and dying. And, this came from a high official in the Governor's Office of Economic Development. Of course, I listened to all opinions. In the end, I did what an Actionaire would do; I followed both my empirical knowledge and my instinctive assessment of the deal.

I saw a hotel with great bones. By this I mean, a potential for greatness. It needed a major overhaul, but the location was breathtaking and unmatched. I knew Detroit had the largest Black American population of any city in the United States and if the hotel was renovated and positioned as a first-class property, with ownership in the hands of a fellow Black American, I surmised it would succeed. With that in mind, I began negotiations with Omni to purchase the hotel.

Omni had the hotel on the market for nearly a year. Offers came and went. Their asking price was high and the property was losing money. I made an all cash, no contingency, offer in late September and it was rejected because they had higher offers. Those offers looked good but had little substance behind them. In October the hotel closed and was boarded up. The utilities remained on and security was there 24 hours a day. Winter was setting in quickly and Omni continued to incur costs and risk. I used all these points to my advantage. Once again I made an all cash, as is where is, offer with an immediate 10 day or as soon as possible closing. They accepted my offer. I then closed the purchase in November 2010.

Now that I owned the property, I immediately began brining in my senior staff to carve out a plan for reopening the hotel. We all agreed that a spring opening would be best. Let the winter be the time for renovation and planning. I also wanted to learn more about the incentives offered by the city and county for new business owners. As a former Alderman in St. Louis, I knew my way around a city hall.

First, I introduced myself to the city council and the mayor. I then learned of a very low interest loan program with no interest or payments in the first year, to assist in the redevelopment of the property. A real estate tax program was available for new owners entitled, "The Turbo Program". This program allowed for a 50% rebate on taxes paid for five years. Additionally, I learned that if your property is out of service on the date of tax assessment which is December 31st and it is placed in a city land-bank for that day, you will be exempt from paying taxes for the following year. I did both and made certain the new tax assessment would be based off of the lower purchase price of the property. It was made clear that 40% of the purchase price was for personal property and not land or real estate, thus doing two things. First, it reduced the real estate tax to an even lower base price for evaluation and assessment and it placed the used furniture and other personal property into a category for a rapid depreciation. This allowed for a more rapid increased bottom line.

The hotel opened in the spring of 2011 as planned under its new name, *The Roberts Riverwalk Hotel and Residence.*

Like most businesses, we had our highs and lows. Some were personnel challenges and physical property issues. After three years of marginal operations I decided to build an outdoor swimming pool and new conference center. With money in hand we began the permitting process. Detroit needs to welcome all investors and on its surface it does. However, when I went for my permits to build a new pavilion, I was required to go before a citizen City Planning Commission. This commission was for review and made a mere recommendation to the city council for a vote to rezone my property.

Moving quickly, I organized and received the support of all the stakeholders in the properties around the hotel accept for one condominium building that decided they wanted to oppose the construction of a new pavilion. They didn't like the fact I cut some trees down on my property and they wanted me to advise them before doing anything to my property. They wanted to limit the number of people we can have at the hotel. It was amazing to hear how other people could have the audacity to impose themselves on your business.

After nearly a year of overcoming this obstacle, I broke ground for the new conference center in 2015. The reality of this challenge was that I still completed my new pool and two new access entries to the bar and grill and the restaurant from the Detroit River Walk directly into those locations.

I conceived another plan for the hotel during this delay. Given its location on the Detroit River, I decided to innovate and create the first urban resort in America with an non-obscured view of Canada; and considering we have the only outdoor swimming pool on the Detroit Riverwalk, and we are offering exotic poolside food and tropical drinks, while offering a gourmet health based fine restaurant. In addition, we have an entire wellness and fitness center, with an Olympic-size indoor swimming pool and outside golf putting green.

This hotel is now dubbed *The Roberts Riverwalk Hotel and Urban Resort* on the Detroit Riviera.

When the Actionaire goes through the dark places they learn more. It develops purpose and trust. A seed is placed in the earth, a dark place. It may not be easy; it may not make sense. After you go through the valley, beyond the dark places you will see your vision, your dream, and opportunity. You will have to go through the struggle and the mistrust when it's lonely. You must be faithful in the dark places because it will turn into the good.

Sometimes when you go through a loss you need to understand a new relationship will come across your path. When one door closes another will open, if you stay true to your dream even when it's dark. You must know you must go through it, to get to it. If you are always trying to wonder why things are happening, you will never get to your promised land.

An exclamation mark is only a question mark straightened out.

You might be asking yourself, "Is it ever going to get better?" The answer is, "Yes!" Don't quit believing, the exclamation mark is coming your way. People don't stop you, rumors can't stop you, only you can stop you. When you are in a dark place, a disappointment or a feeling of despair, the Actionaire forges through. On the other side there are dreams coming to pass.

You can have a seed on your table for a lifetime, but, only after it is planted it generates and grows into the light. First the seed must be planted as it is a critical part of the process. You may not like the dark place, thinking you are buried. But you are not buried, you are planted. But going through the process, new growth is coming your way.

Be willing to go through the process. There may be dirt all around you, but this is the process. You will have to go through this process to blossom and bear fruit. You will go from a victim to a victor.

Life is measured not by length, but by depth.

The people surrounding David, warned him as to the enormous height of Goliath. David's response, "He's short compared to God!" They then said, "Look how big he is." David responded again by saying, "That makes him an easy target to hit!"

Mediocrity to an Actionaire is like Shakespeare reciting mother goose rhymes. Mediocrity is you not fulfilling your potential.

Life is uncertain, but death is certain. Live your life to your highest potential. Every one of us will fall, but there are some of us living in a lifeless body while we are still breathing. Those are the ones who live in mediocrity.

Consider mediocrity as you living in the same boat as everyone you know. They encourage or insist you to do the same things over and over and never rock the boat. Sit down and do everything you do the same way you have always done it. Stay in your place. Find happiness in your mediocrity. They tell you if you step out the boat you will drown. You will not succeed in that business venture you have always dreamed of achieving. These, so called friends or advisors, are stuck in the mediocrity boat and they want you to not grow and become successful as it will make them look like cowards. They are afraid that if they step outside the boat, they will drown.

An Actionaire is never afraid of drowning. An Actionaire knows how to walk on water. To walk on water is defined as stepping out of the boat of safety, security, and comfort. It requires you to dream and plan on a life beyond the mediocrity of that boat. The Actionaire steps out the boat and becomes a water walker who is filled with confidence, courage, bravado, and strategic thoughts. She has a vision for her future and a level of confidence that lifts her out of the boat of mediocrity and placed her on a path to create a new and refreshing quality of life.

While the others in the boat are saying, "Don't step out the boat, you will drown, you will die!" The Actionaire responds with these words, "Perhaps, but everyone in this boat will die one day." Why live your life in mediocrity when you can live a life of fun challenges, expanding ideas, a higher quality of life, and experience change.

Are you in a boat? Are you afraid of change? Do you have a dream but fear failure? Become an Actionaire. Step out the boat and become a water walker. You will find the stones to step on in the water. You can free yourself from mediocrity. If you rock the boat as you step out, it may be just what others who are watching you need to feel and see. It could awaken them from their fears and put them on the path to becoming an Actionaire.

If you step out of this boat of mediocrity on faith in yourself, if you want to control the changes in your life, then change is inevitable. Either you will control those changes or they will control you. As an Actionaire, you are a true water walker and now you are in control of those changes in your life.

Time to Take Action

CHAPTER 12 – BUILD YOUR OWN FENCE

1. What will you do to Build Your Own Fence in your life and business?

   _____
   _____
   _____
   _____
   _____
   _____
   _____
   _____
   _____

2. How will you remain faithful to your goals when the dark times surface in your personal life and/or business?

   _____
   _____
   _____
   _____
   _____
   _____
   _____
   _____

3. What is your vision for your future?

4. How do you face change?

5. How will you fulfill your dreams and eliminate the fear of failure?

_____

_____

_____

_____

_____

_____

_____

_____

_____

Chapter 13

HUMAN TECHNOLOGY

An Actionaire is a Futurist. If your business is to succeed, you must anticipate changes being formulated through Science and Technology. How will these new directions impact your business and your life? It might seem irrelevant or not applicable to you or your company, however, an Actionaire remains informed and explores the innovations taking place globally.

This chapter was written to give you an example of what an Actionaire considers important to observe. Let's peer into the future. What is Artificial Intelligence and Machine Learning? What are their impacts on the human species?

We are in the midst of a revolution of digitalization, capturing all information existing globally. With the creation of an Exabyte, which is a unit of information equal to one quintillion bytes, we have nearly unlimited data capturing capability.

Here is an example of what that means. The Library of Congress has the most books of any library in the world. These books can be stored on one Exabyte 100 times. In 2018, there was an exchange of information across the internet using 1,100 Exabytes. This would be the equivalent of 110 million times the content of the Library of Congress.

The smartphone of 2018 had access to that information which far exceeds that which NASA had when it launched its rocket to the moon. Today's conventional computing technology can be explained having the ability to read one book at a time. Now compare that to the next generation of computing known as Quantum Computing which can read every book in the library at once.

Science and Technology are looking at multiple orders of magnitude growing day by day. This is what is known as Artificial Intelligence (AI). AI is defined as a branch of computer science that develops machines and software with human-like intelligence. It is the theory and development of computer systems able to perform tasks that normally require human intelligence, namely, visual perception, speech recognition, decision-making, and translation between languages.

Machine learning is an application of AI. It provides systems the ability to automatically learn and improve from experience without being explicitly programmed. Machine learning focuses on the development of computer programs that can access data and use what it has learned for itself.

The process of learning begins with observations or data on the order of examples, direct experience, or instruction. The machine then looks for patterns in data and makes smarter decisions in the future. These data are based on what we humans provide. The planned direction of this is to allow the computers to learn automatically without human intervention or assistance and adjust Actions accordingly.

This actually means the machines are coming and we need to understand the obvious consequences of this new technology. It started harmlessly with the auto factories moving out human workers for robotic arms. This points to the job loss that will be inevitable moving forward. Drones delivering pizzas and autonomous vehicle transport removing the human taxi driver's job. Science fiction has been with us for decades and since the 1920s in movies. Today, what has been imagined in film and novels are with us now.

Computers have been around for years. However, the rise of Quantum computing allows us to evaluate the more complex problems facing the human. Quicker computing leads to faster innovation which helps solve difficult problems, i.e. curing diseases, replacing body parts with 3D technology, identifying alternative energy sources, or eliminating hunger.

"Change alone is external, perpetual, and immortal." says Arthur Schopenhauer.

Change is going to happen. The Actionaire refuses to just sit idly by and do nothing, learn nil, and accepts what comes about. Rather the Actionaire's philosophy is to ride the train and not just jump in front of it.

Now where do we go from here? Human-machine collaboration must occur with terms specific to the human. Let's call that Human Intelligence or HI. Machines don't have human traits. They don't have empathy, creativity, critical thought, happiness, cognition, emotion, perception, sadness and they don't love.

The human has a living brain. Our brain has not physically changed since pre-historic times. Our brain is extremely elastic. The human brain is the command center for the human nervous system. It receives signals from the body's sensory organs and outputs information to the muscles. The human brain has the same basic structure as other mammal brains but is larger in relation to the body size than brains in experimental rats and monkeys.

The human brain contains about 86 billion nerve cells or neurons sometimes called the gray matter. It contains billions of nerve fibers also known as white matter. These neurons are connected by trillions of connections or synapses. The forebrain is known as the cerebrum. The cerebral cortex is the largest portion of the brain and is where complex thought and creative thinking originates.

Will HI and AI ever merge and create a super human with the capacity of machine learning? Will there be this singularity of universal thought or a full emergence of technology within the human brain? Today our brain is programmed to accept Virtual Reality (VR) games and trips through VR head devices. Once we are fully immersed into technology, will our brain take us to an augmented reality where imagination appears as reality?

Science and Technology has merged many times over. There are machines and devices that are attempting to capture your dreams through recording your brain waves then converting them into viewing patterns. This is done by recording the brain wave while you are dreaming then waking you up at that moment and have the patient describe what was remembered about the dream.

Let's go deeper, what if all your personal experiences and knowledge could be recorded. Then, via holographic technology, your great, great grandchildren could see you and ask you questions, as if you were literally in front of them. By the way, those children will know very little about driving a car. They will grow up only commanding their autonomous vehicle.

Science and micro technologist are experimenting with wireless brain chips. They placed a wireless communicating brain chip in a rat's brain. The rat was placed in a maze and had to make it through to find its food reward. This rat memorized the path and was able to repeat it. They then placed a brain chip in another rat's brain, miles away at a different location and through a form of telephony or the internet, the learned knowledge of the first rat was sent to the second rat's chip which enabled that second rat to walk the maze exactly as the first rat.

This mind to mind communications offers the possibility, that there will be a transfer of memories, experiences, and all knowledge provided by the internet.

Nano communication chips will be the size of a coffee grain. One day these chips will connect our brains to the internet or directly to the cloud. It will give us access to all public storage of data available on the net. Actual memories and experiences of other people will be downloaded into your brain chip upon request.

Let's go deeper. One day similar nano chips will be inexpensive and you will have them throughout your home and they will be communication-based. Imagine having the chip on your mirror. You wake up feeling bad and you look at your mirror and say, "Mirror, mirror on the wall, what's wrong with me?" Those chips will be able to diagnose your blood pressure problem. Once diagnosed, the chips will send its results to your Robo Doctor who will determine the drug needed to help you. The Robo Doctor will then send the drug request to the Robo Pharmacist who will pull the prescription. Once ready for pick up, a drone company will be commissioned to deliver your prescription to your home. Your Robo Butler will bring the medicine to you along with a glass of Alkaline Water for your consumption.

In the future, there may no longer be a need of Universities as we know them. All information will be on demand. All of us will be smarter with infinite knowledge and storage. There will no longer be isolated individuals as we will be connected to everyone. Today the human has five senses. They are touch, sight, hearing, smell, and taste. The sensing organs associated with each sense sends information to the brain to help the human understand and perceive the world around them. However, with brain chips connected to sensors and data worldwide the human will have millions of senses.

As pointed out earlier, human brains are programmed through current Virtual Reality (VR) units causing experiences and involvement to seem real. Dreams one day, will feel real and can be repeated. Technology will download these experiences and the human will feel like they are there. The brain will be stimulated to take the human in any desired direction.

What else will change in our future? We will be able to live the lives of other people. You will share their emotions, their experiences, and even their pain. Imagine experiencing sky diving, deep sea fishing, or snow skiing in the comfort of your own mind. How about sharing a trip in outer space or walking the Great Wall of China?

Could leaving your everyday life transform you into a state of Nirvana or Heaven, as projected to be the final all knowing existence according to most religious doctrines. We will escape our body and move into a state of all inclusiveness with all human thought and knowledge. Consider how we use our cellular phones now. They are our link to all available knowledge on the net. Now place that capability in your brain. This is placing us on the cusp of some great and challenging issues.

At this point I have taken you to Heaven, but we have to watch out for Hell. Just like our phones and computers can be hacked, brain hackers may surface from the dark side of technology. It's reasonable to believe that these hackers could take control of you without you realizing it, causing you to do things you would never consider doing. Now that would be HELL.

The brain is a generalist. It doesn't break down unless there is the assistance of a hallucinogen, a mentally related disease or a blow from an accident. A machine is a specialist, its basic function is input, processing, and output. However, computers do break down. Let's imagine the delivery of a specialist data into your generalist brain. That would provide you with deep learning and even deeper and more profound understanding.

An Actionaire would be excited to lead in this innovative and great time in human history. We may be the last generation of off line humans.

Complex research into the maintenance of the genome integrity and studying the human DNA could lead to the prevention of breast cancer, Alzheimer's, and potentially aging. With the advent of Quantum computing, our species will become a super human at the level of machine intelligence and that could lead to a form of immortality.

Actionaire sends the call to you to become a Futurist Revolutionist. Find the capitalistic opportunities that will surface and fulfill your potential. Action can lead to controlling change. Your potential must be perfected. You must embrace Science and Technology and take a lead position.

Blue Page Divider with "R" logo in the middle insert on line 5

Time to Take Action

CHAPTER 13 – HUMAN TECHNOLOGY

1. What is innovation?

_____
_____
_____

_____
_____
_____
_____
_____
_____

2. How innovative are you?

_____
_____
_____
_____
_____
_____
_____

3. How will the new directions of Science and Technology impact your business and your life?

4. What is Artificial Intelligence and Machine Learning?

5. How will Artificial Intelligence and Machine Learning impact the nature of business in the future?

6. How will you incorporate Artificial Intelligence and Machine Learning into your business model?

7. If you are to be an innovator, you must take inventory of yourself.

a. What can you do that will be helpful to a customer or potential client?

b. What do you enjoy doing?

c. How innovative would you be if you could eliminate the fear of failure?

Chapter 14
BARTERING TO CRYPTOCURRENCY

If the Actionaire is to stay engaged in all future elements of business understanding world currencies and its changes are vital. So this chapter begs the question. What is currency and how does it change? Money is currency. Money has been a part of human history for more than 4,000 years. It began with bartering and evolved to modern money and now it has evolved to cryptocurrency. How did this system evolve?

From the beginning of mankind, bartering was used instead of money to buy food and other goods. As early as 9000 BC, humans would rear domestic livestock and farmed for food. When they had a surplus, they would then begin the bartering process for those domestic animals, grains, fruits, and vegetables. Bartering was first recorded in ancient North Africa concentrated along the lower reaches of the Nile River. This is now known as Egypt. The success of ancient Egyptian civilization came partly from its ability to adapt to the conditions of the Nile River valley for agriculture. By controlling the floods of the Nile they were able to create controlled irrigation of the fertile valley which in turn produced surplus crops. This supported a growing population and trade culture. Egypt's writing system would be the first to document trade transactions.

Around 1100 BC the Chinese started using small relics of goods cast from bronze. This currency was a trade device which could identify the actual products being exchanged. Coastal people around the Indian Ocean started Cowrie Shells in trade around 1200 BC.

History claims the first known minted coin currency was created in 600 BC. This first coin came from an area in Turkey and featured a roaring lion. Coins then evolved into bank notes around 1661 AD. The first credit card was introduced in 1946; it was called the "Charg-It" Credit Card.

In 1999, European banking began offering mobile banking with the early smart phones. By 2008, for the first time, no contact payment cards were issued in the United Kingdom.

In 2014, Apple announced Apple Pay for their iPhone users. Apple Pay is an E-commerce payment system. Apple Pay allows users the ability to pay for products and services through their headsets. E-commerce payment systems facilitate the acceptance of electronic payment for online transactions. It is also known as an Electronic Data Interchange. The speed and simplicity with which cyber-transactions accounts can be established and used, have contributed to their widespread use. Although the risk of abuse, theft, and other problems remain, these deficiencies allow for bad behavior by the users and criminal hackers. Despite these deficiencies, since 2014, Pushpay, PayPal, Cash App, Givelify App, and many other wireless telephony and online methods have been introduced to the market.

History has gone full circle with the Bartercard. This offers a platform for businesses to barter surplus goods and services worldwide.

Now, the Bitcoin has entered the mainstream of business. It is the first fully implemented decentralized cryptocurrency. I have heard people confusing Bitcoin and blockchain as the same thing.

They are not. However, they are closely related. When the Bitcoin was released as open source code, blockchain was wrapped up together with it in the same solution. Since Bitcoin was the first application of blockchain, people often inadvertently used Bitcoin, the word, to mean blockchain. That's how the misunderstanding started. Blockchain technology has since been adapted for use in other industries. I want all Actionaires to learn the importance of Blockchain Technology. It will be the future of data gathering and securing transactions.

Much like the internet changed the world by providing cloud access to information, blockchain is poised to change how people do business. It is best summed up in one word, "trust". It was designed to have anything recorded on a blockchain to be immutable. It cannot be altered and there are records of where each asset has been. In short, while participants in a business transaction might not be able to trust each other, they can trust the blockchain. The benefits of blockchain for business are many, including saving time to find information, settling disputes, and verifying transactions. It reduces costs and alleviates risk. It therefore, blocks collusion, tampering, and fraud. It can also reduce your overhead and intermediaries such as title companies, lawyers, and banks. Blockchain is only at the beginning of its use in business, politics, and cryptocurrency exchange.

Bitcoin is a type of unregulated digital currency that was first created by Satoshi Nakamoto in 2008. It was launched with the intention to bypass government currency and simplify online transactions by getting rid of third-party payment processing intermediaries. In addition to just making this a form of money, there had to be a secure way to make transactions with the cryptocurrency. Bitcoin transactions are stored and transferred using a distributed ledger on a peer-to-peer network that is open, public, and anonymous.

Blockchain is the basic technology that maintains the Bitcoin transaction ledger.

The Bitcoin blockchain in its simplest form is a data or ledger comprised of Bitcoin transaction records. This database is distributed across a peer-to-peer network and is without a central authority. Network participants must agree on the validity of transactions before they can be recorded. This agreement, which is known as "consensus", is achieved through a process called "mining". I am one who does this mining via machines that teams with a network of other mining locations throughout the world, seeking and competing to handle transactions. Once someone uses Bitcoins, miners engage in complex, resource-intense computational equations to verify the legitimacy of the transaction. Through mining, a 'proof of work' that meets certain requirements is created. To be considered a valid transaction, the blockchain, an individual record must have a proof of work to show that consensus was achieved. By this design, transaction records cannot be tampered with or changed after they have been added to the blockchain. Even if a hacker tried to remove a line in the file, it would be immediately replaced by the other network of computers holding the original data.

Bitcoin thrives due to anonymity. Anyone can look at the Bitcoin ledger and see every transaction that took place, however, the account information is a meaningless sequence of numbers.

You may be asking yourself, "Why is it important for an Actionaire to study this chapter?" There are over a thousand cryptocurrencies on the market today. One can invest in any one of them and hold them as an assist just like stocks and bonds. Their value vacillates greatly. The Bitcoin's first value was pennies in 2008. In December 2017, it rose to a high of nearly $19,000. High speculation had it going much higher, perhaps as high as one million dollars per coin. However, shortly after this high, it took a drastic drop to $3,179.

Other high ranking cryptocurrencies such as Ethereum, Ripple, Bitcoin Cash, and Litecoin tracked the Bitcoin fluctuations. The Actionaire must measure the risk of investing in this currency while at the same time staying open to the daily use of the emerging currency in their business.

Time to Take Action

CHAPTER 14 – BARTERING TO CRYPTOCURRENCY

1. How will cryptocurrency change the way business is conducted today?

_____

_____

_____

_____

_____

_____

_____

_____

_____

2. How can cryptocurrency be utilized within your business?

_____

_____

_____

_____

_____

_____

_____

_____

_____

3. Describe how you can utilize blockchain in your business.

_____
_____
_____
_____
_____
_____
_____
_____
_____
_____
_____

FINAL THOUGHTS

To summarize the true competency of an Actionaire is best evaluated through their leadership skills. I ask you how many do you possess and where should you focus on your development? What are those most important leadership skills?

Actionaires and top-level managers are all interested in perfecting the skill they need to become effective. What are those successful skills and competencies that are associated with ownership and management effectiveness?

A core competency for the Actionaire is the ability to make good decisions or lead a good decision-making process. There are better and worse ways to make decisions and a good manager or entrepreneur understands when to make a decision, when to consult subordinates or peers and bring them into the decision-making process, and when it's time to step back and let others decide. Experience and evaluating when decisions resulted in either succeeding or failing is the best way to develop these skills. Actionaires and independent business persons learn more from their mistakes than from their successes.

One of the best predictors of effective leadership is one's Social Intelligence. However, it can be misunderstood or delayed by your personal evaluation. Social Intelligence is very broad, but can best be viewed in terms of evaluating social situations and dynamics, and ability to operate effectively in a variety of social and business situations. I see this Social Intelligence as defined by many social performances and sensitivity to social situations. Social Intelligence is the ability to understand social situations, to play social roles, and to influence others. It involves being able to see others' perspectives and to understand the complex and abstract social norms, or informal "rules" that govern all types of social situations.

Social Intelligence is what some refer to as "street smarts" or "everyday intelligence". The Actionaire believes Social Intelligence may be the most important type of intelligence for leaders. How does this relate to those of you in or aspiring to leadership positions? The good news is that this form of intelligence is pliable. It can be developed. This relates to interpersonal skills, and the more you develop your interpersonal or people skills, the more you will enhance your Emotional and Social Intelligences.

These are critically important for an Actionaire to be an effective leader. This is a skill that can be developed. You must expose yourself to different people, different social situations, and work to develop your social perceptiveness and ability to engage others in conversation. In my first book, *Action Has No Season: Strategies and Secrets to Gaining Wealth and Authority*, I refer to the value of "small talk" which I now call "Emotional Intelligence Conversations". Also, practice "studying" others' nonverbal signals, particularly signs of emotion. Learn to regulate and control your emotions and your emotional outbursts. Rehearse expressing feelings and become an effective emotional "character". In other words, learn how to express emotions appropriately.

Social and Emotional Intelligence is the ability to communicate with others at an emotional level, to use emotions to help guide the decision making process. The goal is to be able to regulate emotions and possessing knowledge through the emotional processes. This

Emotional Intelligence relates to leadership to some extent. It is important for creating good relationships between the Actionaire and their followers. Charismatic leaders have an extraordinary ability to communicate at the emotional level. Note, however, the use of Emotional Intelligence within the Actionaire is significant but small.

Interpersonal skills could be defined as a subset of Social Intelligence, but these are the more relationship-oriented aspects of social effectiveness. The Actionaire has viewed these as their "quiet skills". They are best represented by interpersonal skills. The best way to develop these interpersonal skills is by becoming a silent listener. You should at the same time perfect your speaking and conversational techniques. Practice with your family, friends, and close associates. You will find that these same skills will materialize into your entrepreneurial relationships.

Developing wisdom is a great virtue. But how is it acquired? It comes from being able to see other's perspectives and through being open to and considering others' points of view.

Listen to others. Work to be more open and broader minded. Learn to ask for others' opinions and consider them as you choose a business direction. All leaders should have prudence or wisdom. Prudence involves gathering evidence, consulting with others, being objective and reflective before deciding on a course of action. It is particularly important for Actionaires to consult with knowledgeable managers and others. This is involving them in the decision process. This leads to greater acceptance of the decisions.

The Actionaire has fortitude or courage. This is having the courage to take calculated risks, having the courage to stand up for what you believe, and doing the right thing. This takes some effort, but the results are rooted in its development. You must however, hold on to your strong personal values. If you truly value something or someone you will have the courage to stand by your principles. You must work with virtues and how they relate to both ethical and effective leadership. A good leader must be courageous and simply staying the course in an evolving business environment is not courageous. Effective leaders need to be bold. In our rapidly changing world, organizations need to innovate and keep up. Simply staying the course means that you will likely fall behind.

Moderation is a virtue and it involves controlling one's emotions and "appetites". It is lack of moderation or temperance that gets many leaders into trouble. Temperance leads to humility. This is a quality found in the very best Actionaires. Temperance helps leaders admit when they've made mistakes and work to correct them.

Being honest in your dealings or creating integrity involves being fair in leading and in dealing with others. Actionaires should not only treat everyone fairly, but they should not put their own gains over those of others.

A higher order of skill relates to conflict management that involves helping associates avoid or resolve interpersonal conflicts. Actionaires are often called upon to mediate when conflicts arise. This involves having the ability to either avoid or resolve your own conflict situations. The largest part of helping conflicting parties is to find a compromise that each party agrees with. This means finding a win-win outcome which will require each party to be flexible and give up something to finalize the conflict. A seasoned leader makes it possible to help the conflicting parties collaborate or find a middle way between two extreme parties.

In your personal life and the business world, people will try to bend rules, gain allies, and fight for their personal agenda in an effort to get ahead. Life is full of politicking. An Actionaire is an effective political player, who knows how the game is played. They can also manage political behavior so that it does not lead group or organizational dysfunction. One develops their political skills similar to the many of the more highly developed leadership competencies. Political skills are learned through experience and learning about people and social changes.

The Actionaire is a master of social influence. Leadership is about influencing others and being able to wield power effectively and fairly. This requires calling on those soft skills to make you more influential in a leadership role. Once developed, these influence skills are used to make reasoned well thought out arguments.

Seeing things from another's perspective can help you understand what they want from a negotiation. This will assist you in focusing on a win-win outcome.

All of these competencies are developed through a lifelong process. An Actionaire gains expertise and competence and tries to learn as much as they can about their organization and their team members. As you face the world of high tech industries or creative firms, you may notice that team members may have more relevant knowledge and expertise than the leaders. Still, it is important that leaders develop their expertise in the particular situation, organization, or industry in which they lead. Study the organization. Study competitors. Continue your education to the very end.

(Photo 1)

ABOUT THE AUTHOR

Chairman/CEO The Roberts Companies

His Excellency Dr. Michael V. Roberts is the Classic American entrepreneur. Born to middle-class hard working parents. His father, Victor Roberts, served as the Executive Vice President of the Roberts Companies since 1974. He is a WWII Veteran and thirty-nine year US Postal Office employee and his mother Delores Roberts is a Retired School Teacher. Educated in the St. Louis Public School System, he worked his way through college and law school to become one of America's leading businessmen. A born leader and scholar-athlete,

Dr. Roberts was Vice-President of the Student Council in college, founder of his campus Association of Black Collegians, President of Kappa Scroller Pledge Class, served on the Editorial Board of the Student Newspaper, appointed Special Assistant to the College Dean of Students and served as Captain of his Varsity Tennis and Basketball teams that became State Champions. He was inducted into the Lindenwood University Basketball Hall of Fame. While in law school, he was elected to the Student Bar Association. Prior to graduation from law school, he was selected as a participant in special summer study programs at the International Institute of Human Rights, Strasbourg, France (1973); and The Hague Academy of International Law at the World Court, The Hague, Holland (1972 & 1973).

Dr. Roberts received his B.S. Degree from Lindenwood University in 1971 and his Juris Doctorate degree from St. Louis University School of Law in 1974. He is the recipient of Honorary Doctorate of Laws Degrees from Lindenwood University and Morris-Brown College. Additionally, he has received an Honorary Doctor of Humane Letters from Tougaloo College.

Throughout his rise in business, which officially started in 1974, Dr. Roberts, along with his brother and business partner, Steven, maintained a strong commitment to the Black American community from which he came. Locating his headquarters in the heart of St. Louis' inner-city, his endeavors over the last forty-five years have created over 11,000 jobs and entrepreneurial opportunities, raised the level of economic activity, and enhanced the quality of life for the Black American community in cities throughout the United States of America.

Dr. Roberts' broad range of professional knowledge and experience developed as both a business owner and an elected public official (St. Louis Board of Alderman, 1977-1985) encompasses the application of innovative financing strategies for large public projects, public-private sector development, negotiation strategies and successful management techniques for urban commercial properties. His leadership in the creation of innovative strategies for financing of redevelopment projects propelled the City into a major redevelopment phase. He sponsored legislation for St. Louis' new convention center, for the historic Fox Theater, the St. Louis Convention Center and Union Station redevelopment. He also was responsible for renaming several streets after famous Black Americans such as the famous Negro Baseball League super star "James Cool Papa Bell".

In the decades that followed his political life, Dr. Roberts used his extraordinary and creative leadership abilities to build a business empire that encompassed television stations, radio broadcasting, commercial, retail, and residential real estate development, a wireless communications company, and owned and managed several hotels. An overview of his achievements includes:

1. Owned & managed 12 full power TV stations. This was the largest Black American owned television group in the United States
2. Owned & managed 13 hotels. This was the largest Black American owned hotel group in the United States.
3. Owned & managed over 5 million sq. ft. of commercial and residential real estate including three city blocks in downtown St. Louis and 20 city blocks in North St. Louis.
4. Largest Black American Residential Real Estate Developer in the Bahamas.
5. Built and operated a PCS digital wireless company. An affiliate of Sprint.
6. Actively participated in taking 3 companies public.

Awards and Recognitions

2019 African American Businessman of the Year Award – NAACP East St. Louis

2019 Community Legend Award – Charlotte, NC

2019 Lifetime Achievement Award MBE Magazine

2019 Global 1000 Speaking Award

2019 Clark University Business School Appreciation Recognition

2019 K.E.Y.S. Community Award Baltimore, MD

2018 Project We Are Free Foundation World Changer Award

2018 Outstanding Service Award Detroit, MI

2017 Project We Are Free Foundation World Changer Award

2017 Business Titan Award by the Dudley Foundation

2016 Best Live Entertainment Award - Detroit Black Music Awards

2016 Distinguished Entrepreneur Award Detroit City Council

2015 St. Louis Police Award for Service to the Community

2014 Outstanding Service to Detroit Business Community Native Detroiter Magazine

2014 Junior Achievement of Greater St. Louis, Business Hall of Fame

2014 United Nations Ambassador & Chaplain at Large - World Life Ministries

2013 Four Eagle Award - Muslim Inaugural Crime

2012 Morehouse College Lifetime Achievement Award - Atlanta, GA

2012 The Grio's 100 Award

2011 Honorary Doctor of Humane Letters Lindenwood University, St. Louis

2011 Marcus Garvey Award - Jamaica, W.I.

2011 Laurel Wreath Recipient Kappa Alpha Psi Fraternity Incorporated

2010 Alabama A & M Appreciation Award

2009 Trumpet Award for Business - Atlanta, GA

2008 Top 25 African-American Businesses in the St. Louis Areas RCGA, Urban League & St. Louis American Newspaper
2008 St. Louis Argus Legend Award St Louis Argus Newspaper
2008 Recognition Award - National Real Estate Brokers Association
2008 Sodexo Lifetime Achievement Award - St. Louis Gateway Foundation
2008 Distinguished Leader: ML King Jr. International Board of Renaissance Leaders - Morehouse College
2008 Outstanding Redevelopment Project Missouri Preservation Commission
2007 Ernst and Young Entrepreneur of the Year
2007 Apex Award for Distinguished Service BM & T Bank
2007 Lifetime Achievement Award for Service, Leadership & Dedication EEI CEO Roundtable
2007 Top 25 African-American Businesses in St. Louis Area - RCGA Urban League & St. Louis American Newspaper
2006 Outstanding Achievement Intercontinental Hotels Group
2006 Recognition of Achievement - Montgomery, Alabama Area Chamber of Commerce
2006 Minority Excellence Award UAW Locals 136 & 597
2006 Communications Alumnus of the Year Lindenwood University
2006 Top 25 African-American Businesses in St. Louis Area RCGA Urban League & St. Louis American Newspaper
2006 Honorary Associate in Arts Degree St. Louis Community College
2006 NABHOOD Leadership Award National Association of Black Hotel Owners, Operators & Developers
2006 Junior Achievement Hall of Fame Junior Achievement
2006 Key to the City of St. Louis, MO Mayor of the City

2006 Beta Gamma Sigma Wisdom and Earnestness Award Texas Southern University
2006 St. Louis Walk of Fame St. Louis Gateway Foundation
2005 Top 25 African-American Businesses in the St. Louis Area RCGA Urban League & St. Louis American Newspaper
2004 Community Leadership Award St. Louis Bar Foundation
2004 Downtown Loft Developer of the Year City of St. Louis
2003 Top 25 African-American Businesses in the St. Louis Area RCGA Urban League & St. Louis American Newspaper
2002 Crescent Award Muhammad Mosque #28

Dr. Roberts was selected as a participant in some of our country's most prestigious programs:

- People to People International Program, Brazil 1981
- Citizen Ambassador Program, Securities Delegation to China 1996
- Army War College, 2001
- Joint Civilian Orientation Conference (JCOC) '75 tour of the U.S. Military Southern Command, 2008
- Federal Communications Commission (FCC) Diversity Advisory Committee
- Appointed by President Obama to the National Advisory Council on Innovation and Entrepreneurship

Dr. Roberts currently serves, or has served on the Board of Directors of the following organizations:

- International Council of Shopping Centers, Trustee
- National Association of Black Hotel Owners, Operators & Developers – Chairman

- National Association of Black Owned Broadcasters
- New Birth Missionary Baptist Church, Atlanta, GA

As a Trustee of the International Council of Shopping Centers, Dr. Roberts has been selected to participate in International Business Tours to Dubai, the Emirates, Johannesburg, and Cape Town, South Africa, Cancun, Mexico, and Toronto Canada. Additionally, as a Board and Faculty Member of the Fraser Power Network, travels have included Ghana, Egypt and Israel.

Dr. Roberts has been the subject of feature stories in the following print and broadcast publications including, but not limited to:

- Atlanta Business Journal
- Black Enterprise Magazine
- Black Meetings & Tourism Magazine
- Business Week
- Daily Times Leader of West Point, MS
- Detroiter Magazine
- Ebony Magazine
- Forbes Magazine
- Kappa Alpha Psi Journal (cover story)
- Milwaukee Journal
- Men's Business Quarterly
- Success Magazine
- St. Louis Commerce Magazine (cover story)
- The Black Collegian Magazine
- St. Louis American Newspaper Newspaper
- St. Louis Business Journal
- St. Louis Post Dispatch
- Urban Influence Magazine

- US Department of Transportation, "Transportation Link"
- Who's Who in Black St. Louis, Author of Introduction to 2009 Edition

Broadcast Features:

- PBS' Nightly Business Report
- CNN
- Fox Business News
- Steve Harvey Talk Show
- Warren Ballentine Talk Show
- Rev. Al Sharpton Talk Show
- Willie Jolly Talk Show
- Michael Eric Dyson Talk Show
- CBS Nightly News
- Featured Guest on Loretta McNary TV Show, Memphis
- Numerous local radio and TV shows throughout the United States and the Bahamas

Dr. Roberts is a high demand keynote business motivational speaker who has been heard by thousands of people from university commencements to not for profit fundraisers, and from community neighborhood groups to corporate boardrooms. His first book, *Action Has No Season: Strategies and Secrets to Gaining Wealth & Authority* is a best seller and very popular with college students and entrepreneurs needing advice on growing their business.

PROSPERITY & ABUNDANCE

**This is a transcript of a 2019 speech given
by Dr. Michael V Roberts, Sr.**

I believe we are all born with a Spirit of purpose and vision. It's up to the Actionaire to develop the skills necessary to experience their purpose and bring their vision to life. We are dreamers. We dream about where we want to be and where we should be but the question is, are we taking Action to fulfill our dreams? If you're going to dream, what's the first thing you have to do to start taking Action? First, you have to wake up, don't you? Then you need to sit up, then stand up, and for those who want to discourage you, tell them to shut up and get out of the way. Actionaires are people who are interested in standing up and taking Action. If nothing else, just stand and believe in yourself and your future.

I know some of you may not have heard of Michael V. Roberts before or my brother and business partner, Steven Roberts. Do you want to know why? It's because rich people scream and wealthy people whisper. My daddy worked at the post office for 39 years. We were not born with a silver spoon in our mouths, I think we were born with a plastic spoon. My mother raised us. There were four children and I remember in the summers, my daddy would not allow me to work at the post office, because he did not want me to get lulled into a position that said, "Here's a nice job and here's a little money for you." I had to work. However, I had to go out and find those jobs. In the summers, I would have two or three jobs, I went to summer school, and I worked my way through school. I was making sure that I didn't put any financial pressure on my parents because I knew my younger siblings were coming behind me.

Ultimately, I graduated from law school. I studied at not only St. Louis University Law School where I graduated, but also at The Hague Academy of International Law School, The Hague Holland at the Peace Palace, The International Court of Justice, and The International Institute of Human Rights in Strasbourg. I want to tell you about a very moving week that has impacted my life and will remain in my memory forever. The very week that I graduated from law school, my brother graduated from college, and he went on to attend law school. During that same week, my mother graduated from college and received her degree after spending years raising her children. I was the oldest, my brother Steven was next, we had another brother, Mark, and then a sister, Lori. It's special for parents to take the time to raise their children. We didn't have great wealth. In fact, we weren't rich and we weren't poor, we just never had any money. However, we were raised to have confidence and courage.

I wrote my first book titled, *Action Has No Season: Strategies and Secrets to Gaining Wealth and Authority,* in it I coined the word, *Actionaire*. The *Actionaire* is someone who sees and understands their vision, their ideas, their dreams, and their purpose and passion; and they pursue it with courage, confidence, and bravado. I hope someday it ends up in *Webster's Dictionary or Wikipedia.* It would be great if Black people had a nice word like that in Webster's Dictionary. Usually, words like "bling, bling" and "bootylicious" get in the dictionary from our culture, but I want us to start to change that.

One of the great things about being worth hundreds of millions of dollars, self-made, is that a brother like me will stand up and say just about anything he wants and he will do it with courage, confidence, and bravado. Brothers and sisters like me, who have made hundreds of millions of dollars don't need to sit back after succeeding. We need to come out and we need to let you hear from us. We need to set the type of examples for young people so that young people can realize that they can become multi, multi-millionaires and they don't have to bounce a ball, they don't have to rap, and they don't have to be illegal pharmacists.

I have four children, the older two, Michael and Jeanne are twins. They graduated from Morehouse College and Spelman College. They were the first boy – girl twins to graduate together Cum Laude on time from those schools. They went on to law school immediately after just like their daddy and their uncle. They completed law school after three years. My daughter Fallon, finished at University of Southern California and completed Pepperdine Law School. My youngest daughter Meaghan, also graduated from Pepperdine's college and law school. Regardless of what you've read in my books, do not judge me on the hundreds of millions of dollars that I've made, judge me on how I am raising my babies.

My dad at the time was in his late 50s when he retired from the post office, he joined my brother Steve and I in running our newly formed family companies shortly after. When we finished law school, we were elected to city council or as an Alderman for just a couple of years. When all of my friends were moving to the suburbs, I moved 2 blocks from the projects. All of my babies were born there. My son, Mike Jr., says, "Guys, I want you to know something, as a kid, my idea of a swimming pool was a fire hydrant. Don't act like you don't know what I'm talking about. True story!" We lived there and we fought the drug issues and passed legislation to improve the community. I lived there for 10 years. How do you give back to the community? That's just one of the ways that you can give back. There are a lot of ways, but at that time, I certainly did not have any money. I was a guy who had just finished school and I had a little debt, but I decided what would be important for me was to get into the hood, get into the neighborhood, and work with my people. I wanted to understand the pain and the difficulties, but at the same time provide a level of leadership that was needed. I served my community and as we say, I earned my street credibility. Don't let the light skin fool you.

We understand what it's like in our neighborhoods because we live in our neighborhoods. We also know that our neighborhoods today, those homes that grandma owned, will be the most valuable properties on the face of this earth tomorrow. Don't you leave your community and don't you let other people step into your neighborhoods and take them over because that is the plan. It is a global interest to live in the United States and more specifically to live in our cities.

People from all over the world would like to live where we live today and we are not taking care of our business and our community.

After my daddy retired from 39 years of working for the postal service, he came to help my brother and me run our companies. We had nothing. The salary of a member of the Board of Alderman in 1977 was $7, 500.00. I thought I had it going on, because I had been out of school for 2 years and I decided I wasn't going to work for anybody. I was going to learn about the growth and the importance of establishing the abundant life. I read where Booker T. Washington suggested that a slave never enjoys the fruits of his or her labor. I thought about that for a moment. So when you have a job, what does that make you? I thought if that's the case and I have a job, "Am I enjoying the fruits of my labor or do I need to have equity and ownership in what I do? Do I have the ability to make that happen?" I didn't want to be a slave to the system and it's a lonely question when you are trying to pay bills. It's a difficult challenge as you continue to live your everyday life. But guess what, you have help. I want you all to become great entrepreneurs, business owners, business people, and someday become like me, a cold-blooded capitalist interested in helping the next generation. Oh, that's cold blooded in the Rick James sense.

Think of me as Barnabas, sent to you to deliver this message. No, I'm not a preacher. But I think I have words to be said from a spiritual perspective. I hope that there is an appreciation for what I have to say. I told you my daddy retired from the post office. It's so great to have a retired bureaucrat around because when we tried to pay him, my daddy would not let us pay him a salary. I asked him, "Why not dad?" He said, "Well, it would affect my government pension!" My parents support us in our businesses and we support them. They have taken over 40 cruises. My father is 96 years old and he is as strong mentally as anyone and he still, occasionally, comes to the office to support his babies. Every time, I see him, I give him a hug and he reminds me he loves me.

When my son finished law school, he and his twin sister came back to live in St. Louis. This is just a cute little side story because parents', I know how difficult it can be when your kids go off to school and they may not come back. I remember as my kids were in Atlanta and they called me one day and said, "Daddy, we sure love it here in Atlanta! They have the coolest clubs and the nicest people. We might live in Atlanta some day!" I said, "Great, fine!"

Once they graduated, they moved out to California to attend school at Pepperdine which is on Malibu Beach. They called me after a couple of years and said, "Daddy, we sure do love Malibu

Beach!" I said, "Yea, you're hanging out at my crib out there and you're enjoying the beach. Stay close to the books." A few months before graduation, they called me and said, "Daddy, what are we going to do? What should we do next? and Where will we be better served?" I said, "I don't know, you said you liked Atlanta and then you said you liked Los Angeles." They said, "Well, we do and we did." I said, "Understand one thing you are describing geography to me. Every city you just named will have potholes, police, crime, and McDonald's. Everywhere you go, you will see the same things, but where is your strength? Where is your family? Where do you have the greatest potential? Then I concluded by saying one other thing, Inheritance is a privilege, it is not a right." They returned to St. Louis.

I am proud to say that after a year of practicing with a major law firm, my son is now the head of our hotel group. My daughter is a transactional attorney and severs as our in-house counsel. So that's a little piece of our family.

Let's talk a little bit about you, the businesses you have created, and the kind of examples you have tried to set. When we think about Jesus feeding the multitudes, when it was time for that one fish to be passed out, Jesus made an interesting move. He taught people to fish. I interpret his teaching, as an entrepreneurial move, you don't need to be on welfare and take just one fish. You don't need to even be in a non-paying, low-paying one fish job. You need to be about the business of learning business. You need to learn that what's internal in you is your destiny. It's an opportunity. You were placed here on earth for purposes. Are you living somebody else's destiny or are you living your destiny? Are you too busy trying to please too many people and not pleasing yourself at the same time? Is it about time for you to start taking care of business? Is it time for you to start realizing that you have certain skills and capabilities that you need to start prosecuting?

We have owned 12 hotels. I was the National Chairman of the Board of the National Association of Black Hotel Owners, Operators, and Developers (NABHOOD) for 10 years. I was thinking hotels and why was I thinking hotels? Why did I think about going into the Hospitality and Hotel Industry? Who has always worked in hotels? Whose middle name is hospitality and who is always taking care of people all of their lives for generations? Black Americans and Hispanics have always been about the job of taking care of people.

Here is an interesting statistic, there are about fifty-thousand hotels in the United States. The Asian-American or East Indians, many of which are named Patel, they own almost 48% of all of the hotels in the United States. They've only been doing this for about the last 50 years. We as in Black people own about 250 hotels in the entire United States, yet we spend approximately $62 Billion dollars on hospitality, travel, hotels, and related services. Take a moment to ask yourself, who is taking that money out of our communities? So, what do we as Black Americans need to do to create the abundant life? We need to be about the business of building and owning hotels.

Now that we've established who works in hotels, who have always worked in hotels, and who manages, operate, cook, clean, and sleeps in hotels, we need to position ourselves to be the owners of hotels now. We will do everything we can to take us to the next level of hotel ownership through the leadership in NABHOOD.

Why? There's about 73 million Baby Boomers who are at a point in their life where they are at some level of a career change. Notice I did not say retirement. Why didn't I say retirement? I didn't say retirement because I don't believe in retirement. I believe you should never retire. You should always find your purpose, go after it, and pursue it. One of greatest things we've faced, is when we follow the status quo and we let people tell us to get educated, get a nice job, stay the course, don't rock the boat, do it the way it's always been done, and one day we're going to retire you and send you away with a fake gold Timex Watch. If you don't take Action to build and have your own dream and vision, you'll work your entire life taking forced Action to build someone else's dream.

We are homo sapiens, meaning we are an animal, we are a creature of earth. What would happen if a lion retired? It would become its neighbor's breakfast. You cannot retire ever. You have too many purposes. Notice, I said, purposes, meaning you are here to serve more than one purpose in your lifetime. Everyday when you wake up, you are given 86, 400 seconds. Who's doing the math? That's 24 hours right? The moment that you think of that moment, it's already gone. So either you use your moment or you lose your moment and what's important for you to understand is how you maximize the moment in which you are existing. I say to you that the reason I have so many companies is because I am constantly in movement. I don't believe there is a such thing as retirement. What a mistake that is, you retire at a point when your brain is the strongest, you're the most knowledgeable, and you have more money than you've ever had.

Take Action and start a business. You can start a business at 60, 70, and 80 years old and realize that you can do it. Eighty is the new 50. We have longer life spans. We have the ability to do more. You are the brightest and the best as you have matured into those ages. I also want you to realize that you can start a business at age 16. Somebody asked me, "Michael, when did you start your business?" I said, "I started when, well maybe some of you are old enough to remember when one dollar meant something. My daddy said, "Cut the grass, because it's how you earn your allowance." My allowance was one dollar. I did as I was told and I cut my daddy's grass, but then I cut my neighbor's grass and I was paid five dollars. I was suddenly awakened to the reality of being an entrepreneur and that's how it all started for me. Cutting grass for an allowance was a job, cutting grass for our neighbor was a business.

Give back to the community. Look into our neighborhoods, think about developing our communities, and when you do that, think in terms of building green. Our various businesses in St. Louis have included the construction of Single-Family Homes as well as Condominiums that are energy efficient. There was a school house that was vacant, it was standing there as a monolith to crime and pestilence, and we bought that property. Today, it has 72 brand new fresh units where our people can come in and live a quality of life that is suitable for the earnings that they make out here in the world. We have also built Single-Family Homes that are what I call the New Affordable Living Home. In our homes, they are built Green. We wanted them to be sustainable so that when you put down a floor, it may look like hardwood but it's actually Bamboo. Bamboo grows about a foot a day in some climates. This is far more efficient and prevents us from having to cut down a tree that takes 50 years to grow. We can save our Planet by beginning to make changes today and in our day to day life. It's healthier, it's more productive, and it's an emerging industry that we can all learn about and start to become wealthy from it.

I use the word wealth and I say that frequently in my books. I hear people talk about being rich. What did I say at the beginning, rich people scream but wealthy people whisper? Too frequently, we worry about having power and being rich. Let's go back to my first book, the subtitle is, *Strategies and Secrets to Gaining Wealth and Authority.*

Let's make some fundamental distinctions there. Do you want to be wealthy or do you want to be rich? Too often we get the impression that being rich is what it's all about. Some people are more concerned about having bling in their ears, nose, around their necks, and their toes and they don't have $20 in their pocket. I see women with $5,000 Gucci bags and no money in them. I'd rather see a woman with a plastic bag and $5,000 cash in it. I always thought it strange when someone has a Land Rover vehicle and a Landlord.

Being rich is a one generational scenario. Being wealthy is sustainable. It means you're passing on your legacy of wealth to the next generation. You're passing on your "genes". I want you to learn the importance of generational expansion for us as a people to continue to succeed and prosper.

You want to have sustainability, you want to leave a legacy, and you want an inheritance to pass on from generation to generation. Wealthy people understand this concept. Rich people burn it up in their lifestyle and in their lifetime. We have to be more about the business of providing for the next generation and the next 100 years.

I'm a businessman; I used to be an entrepreneur. An entrepreneur is someone whose business focuses on the expansion and the development of their family business. I am no longer an entrepreneur. Over the years I have employed over 11,000 people and I have companies with assets that were once valued at close to a Billion Dollars. We have done very well. My friend Muhammed Ali once said to me, "Mike, it ain't bragging if you can back it up!" So, I said to him you're absolutely right, but I do believe that I have to follow the philosophy of the great Reverend Ike, who once said, "The best way to help poor folks is to not become one."

Today, I am a cold-blooded capitalist. Don't be afraid of that word. They have tricked us to think that when we live in a Capitalistic Society we're not supposed to be a capitalist. Does that make sense?

We are a capitalist, that means we are about the business of establishing our companies so they will have generational opportunities.

When I travel the globe speaking, as a part of my introduction, a video is played for the audience to give them an overview of some of my many accomplishments. In the video there are highlights of my companies and the names of my companies. Roberts' this and Roberts' that.

Afterwards, somebody came up to me and said, "Mike, what do you have some kind of ego problem?" I said, "No, but what do you have some kind of envy problem? You didn't say that to Mr. Rockefeller, Mr. Dell, or Mr. Ford and as you sip on that 40 bottle, you didn't say that to Mr. Busch or Mr. Coors. Get out of my face man."

We have to think ahead. What may seem like ego today, will be legacy 40 years from now. We have to build legacies and transferable wealth that can last for generations, it's generational. It's a substitute word for gene. It's passing on the gene. That's what we have in us, genetics. We don't always have to rely on Empirical knowledge. You might write a business plan but if you don't have the vision or the instinct, it's not going to work. You might have one that's not as strong but you have the vision and you can see it and you can understand it. Then you can make it work.

We have to think in this new millennium differently than we ever thought before. Why, because there is this emerging convergence of opportunities, global opportunities. Let me give you an example. Let's assume that a hundred years ago, on this very morning, my brother Steven and I in 1907 were leather buggy whip manufacturers. Steven says to me, "Mike, I think I am going to change my leather buggy whip manufacturing business to making leather seat covers for this new thing called the Model T." My response might be, "Steven, nothing is ever going to replace the horse and buggy." Well, who carried the future for the next hundred years.

Think about this for a moment, what if Henry Ford was Henrietta Ford a hundred years ago? How many jobs, how many businesses, or how many people would have been educated as a result of Henrietta's selection of who is in charge of the companies. I'm assuming Henrietta is a sista, by the way. In case you didn't figure that out. Notwithstanding racism and sexism, get that out of the way. Here we are in a new emerging time. The time I just referred to was when we were moving from an Agrarian Society, an Agricultural based Society to an Industrial Society but today we have very interesting dynamics taking place as well. They are the dynamics of creation and formation of new technologies.

Business opportunities are springing up all over the world. As Tom Friedman says in his book, *The World is Flat*, it is flat. You can get online and talk to people in China and anywhere else in the world to sell or buy goods and services. What's happening to us in our world? What's happening to us here in the United States? The clothes you wear today are made in China. Most of the green foods that you eat are grown in South America. The diamonds you wear and chocolate that you eat come from Africa and Europe.

I mentioned earlier that we must start realizing that we have certain skills and capabilities so that we can start prosecuting. Why do you need to go after them? We need to go after them because we live in a Global Society today and that is why your jobs are fungible. Wow, what does that mean? This is sort of a legal term. It means that, at any point your employer can outsource your job to somewhere else like India, China, Cambodia, Russia, Vietnam and all of these places that are enjoying our cash and you will never know what hit you. Today, we are a creditor to no one and we are a debtor to China.

China and others globally are looking to do business with us. They want to be just like us. They want to be westerners.

If you consider what's internal in you and you begin to not just deal with empirical knowledge, that which you've learned in school, at church, and amongst your family and friends, but you will start to realize that you've been blessed with something called Instinct. Instinct is your inner compass, the voice of your spirit that will allow you to get in touch with your flesh. Your instinct is something that is internal to you and it's genetically driven. Realize that it is a continuation from the origin of man.

I wrote about this in my first book, *Action Has No Season: Strategies and Secrets to Gaining Wealth and Authority*, being genetically driven. Now, what exactly is being genetically driven? I was watching these brothers and sisters get out of jail because they found out that their DNA did not match the individual who apparently committed the crime. So, they let them out of jail because the DNA didn't match. What is that? What is DNA? Without being scientific, DNA is a code that is within you. It's the internal understanding that you were given at birth.

Where did it originate? Where did we originate? Where did man originate? What country have we found the oldest individual?

Our origin is Africa. You are a part of a genetic code that's gone on for thousands and thousands of years. This means the power of our Spiritual Father that started us off, started us off where, in Africa. If it started us in Africa and those are our Ancestors, then that means we have a genetic link like no one else. That means there is genetic memory and strengths within you that were provided to you by our Spiritual Father at the beginning of our origin that continues to live on in our spirit, our DNA, and our body. We have capabilities like no one else.

I want you to be in touch with your instincts and let that govern you along with your learned empirical knowledge and let that govern you along with your spiritual feelings. Instinct is really the Holy Spirit. That is what is manifesting you to do things everyday. The same thing that told you, "It's too dark on this side of the street, I better cross over, something is telling me that I need to move over to the other side of the street and leave quickly!", is your instinct. This is that still small voice in your ear speaking to you to guide you like a built-in inner compass. Allow your instinct to play a role in guiding you through your personal life and your business.

I mentioned being genetically driven, when I was a kid, my dad and mother would do things to me and I would say, "When I grow up, I'm not going to do that and I'm not going to treat my kids this way!" The older I get, the more I find myself doing exactly what my parents did. You will find behaviors similar to your parents and your grandparents. But guess what, thousands of people copulated to create you. You go back thousands of years. There's no spontaneous generation. We're not sitting here saying, "Oops, here's somebody new?" You are a part of an unbroken chain and in that chain, there was all types of information and data created to make you who you are.

How often have you felt for a moment and you look at some idea and you said, "Look at that, what an interesting idea, and I had that same idea three years ago." Now someone else has gone out and they've made millions and millions of dollars on your idea. What stood between you and the success was Action. Don't wait to take Action. That is why I wrote the book and entitled it, *Action Has No Season*. It's an existential concept that means you must fulfill every moment to its fullest extent. As stated earlier, everyday when you wake up, you are given 86,400 seconds, that's 24 hours for anybody doing the math. In that time period, you must either use it or you will lose it.

So, I'm asking you today to think not in terms of what's going to happen next week and not what's going to happen far down the road, but realize that you have a personal presence at this moment and at the moment you think of the moment, it's already gone. So if you have an idea for a business or a thought to create some new technology, get on it, get after it, find a way to package it, and find a way to make it happen. Too frequently, people start to think one way and then they limit themselves.

Do you think out of the box? If you said yes, this is when I start to spank people. If you are thinking outside of the box, doesn't that presume that you are in a box? Hold your head and say ouch, if you're in a box, what is the size of your box? Is it the size of this room? Is it the size of a prison cell? I know people and their box is their casket. They never do anything in life. There is no box. There is no such thing as a box. There's only the blessings you receive and those blessings you must take action upon.

If I felt like there was a box, how could I have gone and stood and rang the bell at the New York Stock Exchange (NYSE) when people said, "Black folks don't do that kind of stuff." Let me tell you about trust. When I rang that bell and I looked down on the stock exchange, I saw all of these people moving around, shuffling paper, nodding their heads, and pointing. I didn't see not one dollar changing hands and then I realized that on the New York Stock Exchange, $13 plus Trillion dollars exchanged hands on trust alone. Thirteen Trillion dollars on trust alone. We should be doing business with each other. Why aren't we doing business with each other? Why? Because the system has told us to do it the way it's always been done, don't rock the boat, stay the course, and I'm going to retire you one day from your wonderful little job and reward you with a fake gold Timex watch and send you on your way.

You have the duty and the responsibility in our community to make that happen. So I looked at how we build new homes in the inner-city areas of St. Louis. I found that there was a need for us and we needed to finance our deals. At the time, the bankers were saying they didn't understand the purpose of building a strip shopping center on Dr. Martin Luther King and Kingshighway. Whenever you say, Dr. Martin Luther King in reference to a street in any city in the United States, that already connotates a negative, doesn't it? We have to be about the business of taking our street, Dr. Martin Luther King and doing something with it. I am tired of us sitting back and waiting for somebody else to come in and teach us how to do better when we already know how to do better.

When my brother and I, in trying to build behind the old Sears building in St. Louis, which is now known as the Victor Roberts Building; Why did we name it the Victor Roberts Building? We named it after our daddy because he was in there helping us when we had nothing. As far as we were concerned, all Mr. Sears did was move out of our neighborhoods. We then decided there was a need for new brick in our neighborhood.

We had previously taken two companies public, we were developing great wealth, and yet the bankers because of the neighborhood did not, "understand the model", "the business plan", or "could not evaluate it". In response to this denial, we wrote the $4 Million dollar check ourselves. We built in our neighborhoods and as a result, it is 100% occupied. Afterwards, every bank president was saying, "Oh how brilliant that was!" They all somehow wanted to do business with me. If you want to do business with Mike and Steve

Roberts, our office is on Dr. Martin Luther King and Kingshighway come and see us.

I told you, a brother with a lot of money is just a bad cat. We have to be about the business of making sure that the word continues to spread amongst our family through ancestral DNA. I don't need to wake up early in the morning and do much if I don't want to, but I do because I enjoy it so much. I'm not really impressed with a 40-hour week; I'm looking for a 40-hour day. If you are fulfilling your goals, your visions, your dreams, you can't wait to wake up in the morning. It just burns you to just jump up and get up. It's like coming to church saying, "I just gotta get there!" That's what it's going to take. Make sure you continue contributing to your church, because tithing is a major factor in your success. It is not an option.

You have to protect your base and this is how you do that. What would your life be like if you could eliminate the fear of failure? Think about that for a moment. I'm going to break that down for you because there are two words that I want to talk about. They are, fear and failure. The first word is fear; fear is nothing more than a construct. That means it is something that was formed and defined for you. When you were born, you were born supreme. Say it out loud, "I was born supreme!"

It was after that, that you began to find yourself discovering these things called fear or thinking in and out of the box. I think all of these little phrases are institutionally set up to limit your growth. For me to be successful in my businesses I must eliminate the fear of failure. Fear is not of nature, it is not lightening, it is not the wind, it is not a tornado. Fear is a mental construct. It is only what you allow it to be. If you can eliminate that mental construct. If you can take that and blow it away, you've eliminated fear.

The second word is failure. Failure is nothing. If you look at your

86, 400 seconds, you'll look at them differently now. You're going to take that time and think, "I don't even have time to deal with failure now because everything that I do, every experience is just another opportunity. The experience just did not turn out the way you planned. It doesn't mean that you failed; it just means that you engaged in another experience.

I don't even know what failure is. I know there are times when I've done things and the outcome was not as I would have liked them to have been. That's not failure, that is an experience. You may have relationships, women with some men and you might think that the relationship is a failure. It is not, it is an experience. Men, you have met some women who are not exactly who you expected and it's an experience.

It is not failure, it's the same thing in business. I understand people pretty well, because I am just still the son of a postal employee. I recognize the importance of what it takes to sustain yourself while you're building your businesses. The reason why I am so diversified is because I knew there would be lead times between the beginning and the fulfillment of one of the projects, so I would start little projects. I would plant seeds and I would allow those seeds to be nourished and let them grow. I know I cannot plant an apple seed and expect a stalk of corn to grow. I have to know exactly what I am planning to do. I know that if I'm able to establish the types of businesses that I'm interested in and thinking that, "Wow, there is no such thing as a box, so who's to say that this brother can't own an aviation company, who's to say that he can't own TV stations, and a radio station!"

We were featured in Black Enterprise Magazine about the Roberts' Brothers, you know these two brothers you never heard about. We are the same two brothers who have been written up in Forbes Magazine and have always been in the Top 100 Black Businesses for years. If you didn't know who we were, you've got to read and share the information with your friends and family members.

There's a lot of information out there for us to learn about. I want us to recognize that there is no such thing as failure. There are only experiences. So now, let's eliminate the fear of failure. It's gone. It's gone. Put your hand on your heart and say, "Michael I feel you, I understand what you are saying!" Now, I am able to do some things that otherwise I might not have done at 70 or at 21 years old because I am going to go for it. You're not foolish, but the one thing you want to do is recognize that your goal is to be a part of living the abundant life. Right? Therefore, you have instinct that will help you drive out fear and the fear of failure. We have to come to terms with not being controlled by or consumed with fear.

What is that again? How does Michael Jordan who has parents who are not tall, become one of the greatest basketball players in history? How does a little four-year-old girl get on the piano and play Mahler or Beethoven? They allow their instincts, those things that are a part of their genetic pool to surface and they don't run away from them. They are not afraid to succeed and that's what I want us to do.

With all of the companies that I have, I am trying to get people to understand this definition between power and authority. In our minds, we have always been told that we want to be powerful. I am trying to change that. Why or how? Here's my explanation for this, the most powerful man on the face of this earth at one time, was George W. Bush and previously it was Bill Clinton and for those Georgians, it was even Jimmy Carter at one time. I was an Alderman, I thought I was an extremely powerful person. I could move a stop sign. I could make sure that certain sidewalks got repaired. Boy, I thought I had power.

If the then President Bush were to go to India and Pakistan and say to them, "You guys need to stop this feud you have on your borders, it is potentially creating a global disruption and the type of disruption that could lead to a war." We're only talking about an inch or a mile of real estate. The heads of those two countries would thumb their nose at the most powerful man on the face of the earth and they would say, "This is my motherland. Why don't you just go back to the United States?" At the same time, we are seeing the emergence of a very strong middle-class in India, Pakistan, China, and Cambodia. This is because money from Hewlett-Packard, Dell, Motorola, and other big companies are dropping billions of dollars into these countries. These are the same countries where their kids are coming over to our schools, sitting in the seats where our kids should be sitting, getting educated, and then we don't even have the presence of mind to give them a Green Card. Then they go back to their country and start companies to compete against us for your jobs.

Let's assume for the moment that Michael Dell goes to the heads of India and Pakistan and his words would be, "If you start a war and affect the supply of parts for my computers, I will pull my businesses out of your country and affect your middle class. He has *authority;* Bush has *power*, which one would you rather have? Yes, you would rather have authority. I don't care who the President of the United States is. If Mr. Halliburton and Mr. Bechtel walks in and said, "I want a $10 Billion dollar no bid contract, they're going to get it. If we had to choose between Power and Authority, I want us choosing having authority. It's all a part of how we begin to change as we move into the new century.

As we move into the new century, we want to have a Henrietta Ford. We want to have a Henrietta Ford for the next hundred years, her invention, her concept of BPL, Broadband over Power Lines. What's that? Well, I'm a Futurist and I predicted that someday you would be able to plug your modem into your electric plug and connect your internet using electricity. Why, because light is faster than sound. It's more effective and ultimately, it's more robust. The internet is now being used all over the world. At the same time that I had made that prediction, I also noted that half of the world had still never made a phone call using the internet and look at the opportunities we now have to connect voice conversation via the internet.

When Edison created the light bulb, he had critics and haters. I want to make a point about critics and haters, these people love to find an excuse to try to discount or discredit your vision. I understand that Edison tried a thousand times to get the light bulb to work and his haters were critical of him. When he completed it; people said, "What do you have to say to your critics now?" He didn't say anything, he just walked across the room and turned on the light bulb. That's how we roll! You don't have to waste your time addressing your haters. Stay focused and your Actions will speak for you. We had playa haters in St. Louis for what we were doing. I didn't worry about that. I'd just make them drive by my house and see my Rolls Royce and Aston Martin. A brother has got to have a little bling in his life, right? We have to keep representing.

As we look into the future and we have all of these different business opportunities, there are tremendous gains for us as Black People for the next 100 years. I want us to think in terms of keeping our neighborhoods and building within and not without. Let's look closer to where we are and what we have. Let's also be considerate of the fact that this is now a global economy.

What are the alternative fuel sources? When I look at the definition of Affordable Housing, I don't just think about building a shack and throwing somebody in there. We live in a very gluttonous environment and we use a lot of energy so I think in terms of building homes that are energy efficient. I call these the new Affordable Homes. We build them using Geothermal Heating. That means when we drill down 150 feet next to the home, we're drilling to hit water at a temperature that's approximately 50 degrees, and we use this water to cool the coils of a heat pump. This Geothermal Heating process allows the home to stay at and sustain a set heating or cooling temperature that will allow the monthly bill to stay around $40.00 to $50.00 a month for the rest of the life of that house. That's affordable housing.

So let's start learning how to build our homes efficiently. It is important for us to protect our planet. It is important for us to think long enough and far enough ahead to realize that we can make an impact and make money in the hustle, in the game, or in the opportunity. We can make money and create generational wealth in this emerging concept of energy conservation that is continuously evolving.

Let me just add one final thought to your minds. In the old boy system and notice I did not say the old girl system because there weren't any girls in the system, it's set up to perpetuate itself. It has indoctrinated us to function in a certain way. We can survive but we have to have equity. We have to become homeowners and business owners. If we aren't enjoying the fruits of our labors, we are just modern day slaves.

We have to make sure that our children will have the direction that we can give them through general understanding, knowledge, courage, and confidence. If we can eliminate the fear of failure and we become Actionaires, we take on the position that there is no such thing as a box. When we think about going to church and we think about God, are we thinking about God in a box? No. It is a full robust limitless thought. It's Omnipresent and guess what, so are you. In your hearts and in your minds all you have to do is release and go after your dreams, your vision, your ideas, and pursue them.

Let's accelerate our people into success. Let's make it possible for there to be generational wealth. Let's make it happen. I don't mean giving your kids a deed or an insurance policy when you die. I think that's a mistake. If you have a little business and a home, leave a little debt on it so that they can earn and grow off of your seeds, off of the tree that you've planted. Don't make it so easy that they can just pop up and do their things. I didn't do it with my babies, they have to work. Having a good work ethic is a good thing. It's a thing from the heart, it's smart. It builds strong character. So for us to live the new abundant life of the 21st Century, let's take it on! I just want us to do one important thing, let's change the Old Boy Network and make it the Home Boy and Home Girl Network and that means making more money and living the abundant life for generations to come. Enjoy your new abundant life! Thank you.

Connect With Me!

Website: www.ActionHasNoSeason.com
Email: MichaelVRoberts@ActionHasNoSeason.com
Instagram: @MichaelVRoberts
Twitter: @MichaelVRoberts
Youtube: Michael V Roberts Sr

Made in the USA
Columbia, SC
09 February 2020